Arranged by
BILL BOYD

EASY PIANO

The PHANTOM of the OPERA

Music by ANDREW LLOYD WEBBER
Lyrics by CHARLES HART
Additional lyrics by RICHARD STILGOE
Title song: lyrics by CHARLES HART,
Additional lyrics by RICHARD STILGOE & MIKE BATT
Book by RICHARD STILGOE & ANDREW LLOYD WEBBER

The Phantom played by MICHAEL CRAWFORD
Christine played by SARAH BRIGHTMAN   Raoul played by STEVE BARTON

*You must be always
on your guard,
or he will catch you with his
magical lasso!*

*He's here:
the Phantom of the Opera . . .*

I only wish
I knew your secret!
Who is this new
tutor?

Say you need me
with you,
now and always . . .

Angel of Music!
Guide
and guardian!
Grant to me your
glory!

*And in
this labyrinth,
where night is blind,
the Phantom of the Opera
is there —
inside my mind . . .*

*Let the dream begin,
let your darker side give in
to the power of
the music that I write . . .*

Behold! She is singing to bring down the chandelier!

I advise you to comply —
my instructions should be clear —
Remember,
there are worse things
than a shattered chandelier . . .

Masquerade!
Stop and stare
at the sea of smiles
around you!

Have you missed me, good messieurs?
I have written you an opera!

The world forgot him,
but I never can . . .
For in this darkness
I have seen him again . . .

In sleep
he sang to me,
in dreams
he came . . .
that voice
which calls to me
and speaks
my name . . .

You alone
can make my song take flight . . .

Fear can
turn to love — you'll
learn to see, to
find the man
behind the monster . . .

Andrew Lloyd Webber was born in 1948. He is the composer of *Joseph And The Amazing Technicolor Dreamcoat* (1968) (extended 1972), *Jesus Christ Superstar* (1971), the film scores of *Gumshoe* (1971) and *The Odessa File* (1973), *Jeeves* (1974), *Evita* (1976), *Variations* (1978) and *Tell Me On A Sunday* (1979) combined as *Song And Dance* (1982), *Cats* (1981), *Starlight Express* (1984) and *Requiem*, a setting of the Latin Requiem Mass (1985). Mr Lloyd Webber's awards include three Tonys and the Grammy Award for Best Classical Contemporary Composition for *Requiem* in 1986. *The Phantom of the Opera* won 'Best Musical of 1986' in both the Laurence Olivier and Evening Standard Drama Awards. He is married to Sarah Brightman.

Charles Hart was born in 1961 and educated at Desborough School, Maidenhead, Robinson College, Cambridge and the Guildhall School, London. His first compositions were heard while he was still at school, and he appeared in some thirteen plays, musicals and operas while at university, where he also wrote words and music for a variety of songs and one (unperformed) musical, *Moll Flanders*. Since leaving the Guildhall, where he studied composition with Robert Saxton, he has worked as a keyboard player, répétiteur and vocal coach in the West End. *The Phantom of the Opera* marks his début as a professional stage writer.

Richard Stilgoe has a wife, an ex-wife, five children, a dog and a Hymac digger. From this you will gather that he is passionate and creative but essentially down to earth. He was born in Camberley and brought up in Liverpool, where he sang 'I Know That My Redeemer Liveth' at St. Agnes' Church and 'Rip It Up' at the Cavern. In trying to write a song as good as either of these, he has now written several hundred, and played the results on radio *(Today, Stilgoe's Around* and the prize-winning *Hamburger Weekend),* on television *(Nationwide, That's Life,* his own series and everyone else's) and on stages all over the world. His one-man show has been seen at festivals from Edinburgh to Adelaide. Clients for his bespoke cabaret act include IBM in Rhodes, Butlin's in Toronto and H.M. The Queen at Windsor Castle. His two-man show with Peter Skellern ran happily in London's West End, and is soon to be seen on Broadway. For Andrew Lloyd Webber he co-wrote with Trevor Nunn the words for the opening song of *Cats*, and all of the words in *Starlight Express*. This has paid for the Hymac digger, and enabled him to found the Orpheus Trust, which helps disabled children to play and enjoy music. Much of his work is now with children. He has his own BBC 1 children's series, introduces opera to children at Glyndebourne and is a patron of the National Youth Music Theatre, for whom he is currently writing the words and music of *Bodywork*, a musical that takes place inside the human body. This has its première at the 1987 Brighton Festival, before going on to Edinburgh. He still occasionally sings 'Rip It Up', but now finds 'I Know That My Redeemer Liveth' a bit high.

THINK OF ME

Lyrics by CHARLES HART and RICHARD STILGOE
Music by ANDREW LLOYD WEBBER

Moderately

with pedal

CHRISTINE:

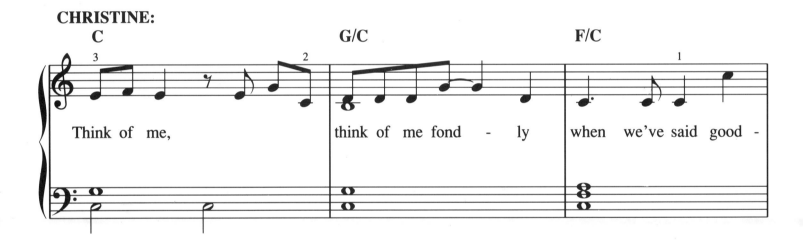

Think of me, think of me fond - ly when we've said good -

bye. Re - mem-ber me ev - 'ry so of - ten

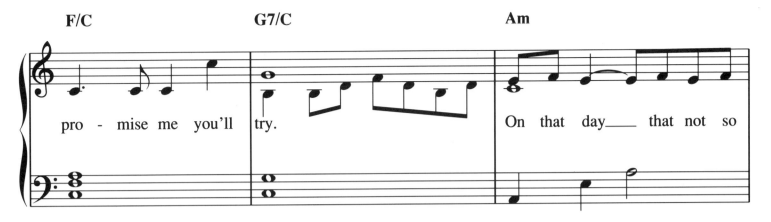

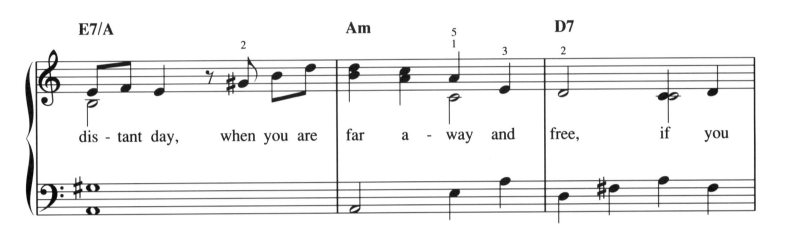

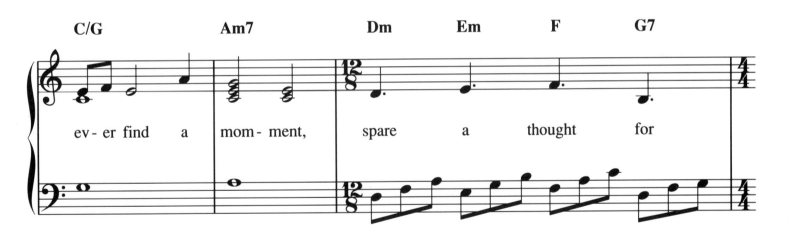

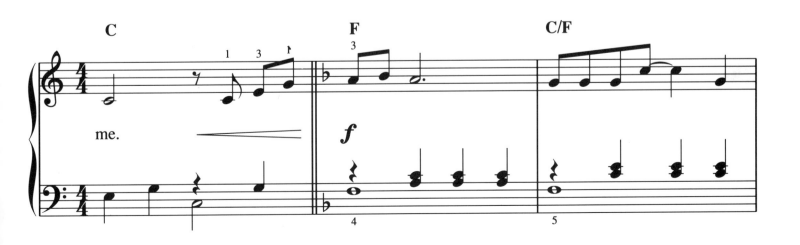

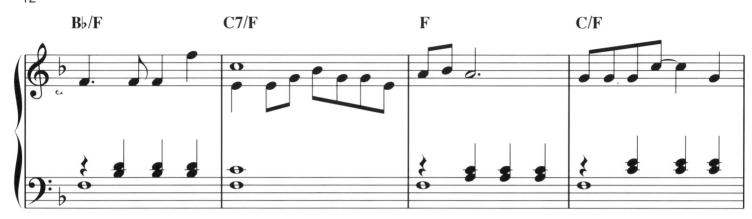

And though it's clear_____ though it was

al - ways clear that this was nev - er meant to be, if you

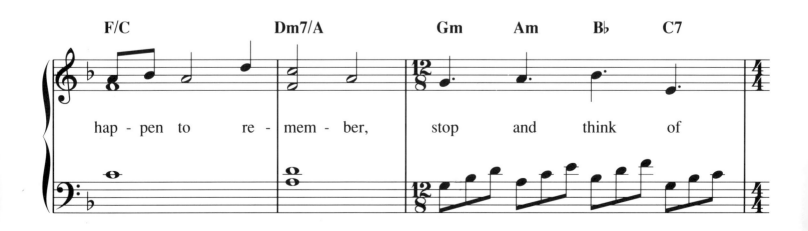

hap - pen to re - mem - ber, stop and think of

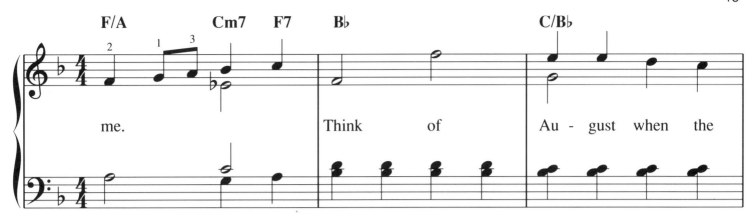

me.   Think of   Au - gust when the

trees   were   green;   don't   think a - bout   the

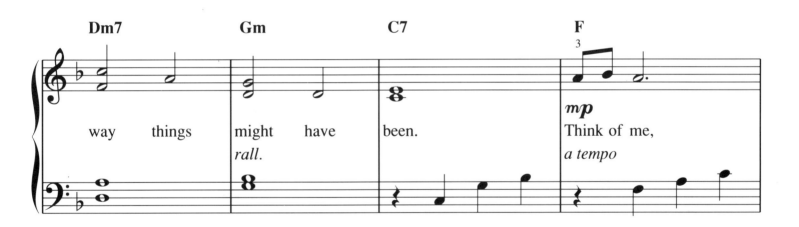

way   things   might   have   been.   Think of me,

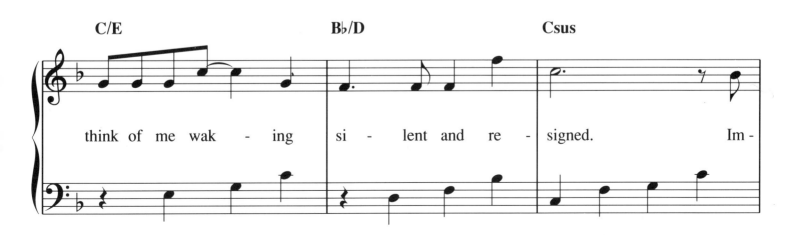

think of me wak - ing   si - lent and re - signed.   Im -

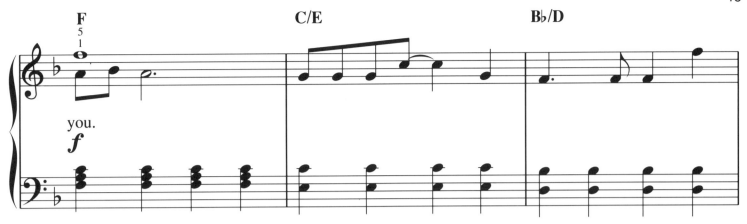

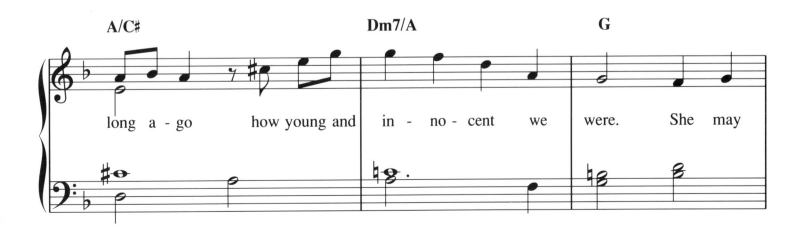

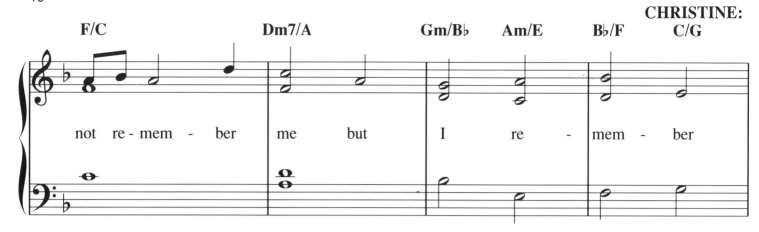

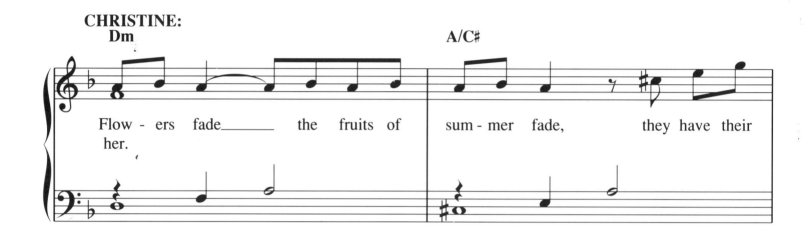

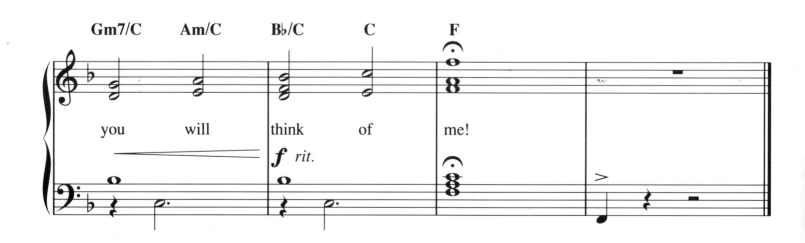

*Think of me,
think of me fondly
when we've said
goodbye . . .*

ANGEL OF MUSIC

Lyrics by CHARLES HART and RICHARD STILGOE
Music by ANDREW LLOYD WEBBER

Slowly (in two)

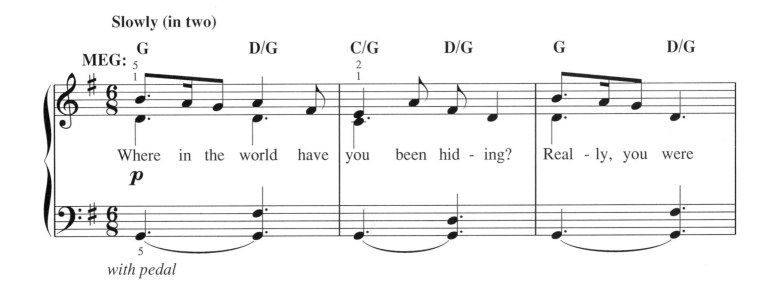

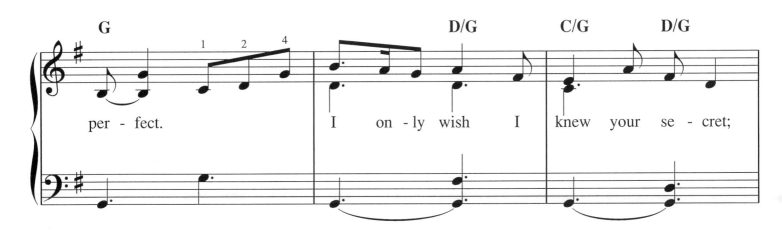

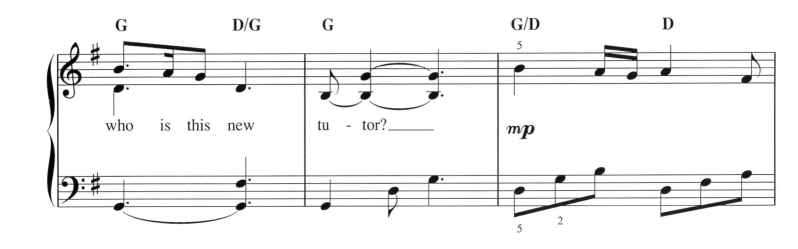

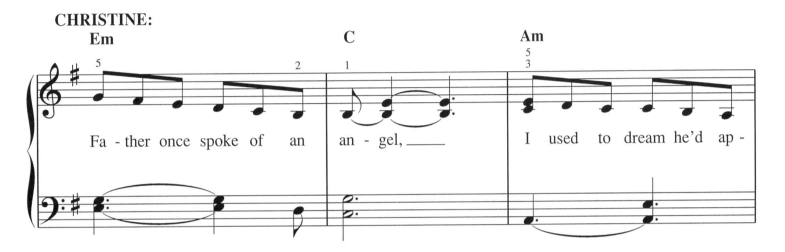

CHRISTINE:

Fa - ther once spoke of an an - gel, _____ I used to dream he'd ap -

pear. Now as I sing I can sense him _____ and I

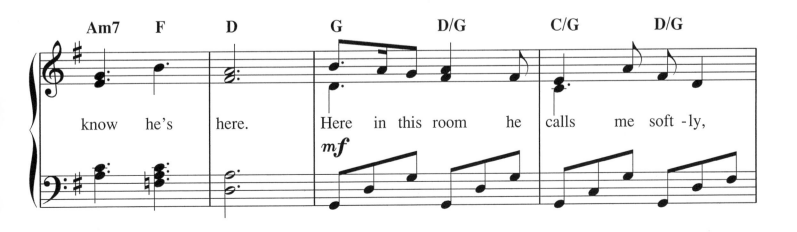

know he's here. Here in this room he calls me soft -ly,

mf

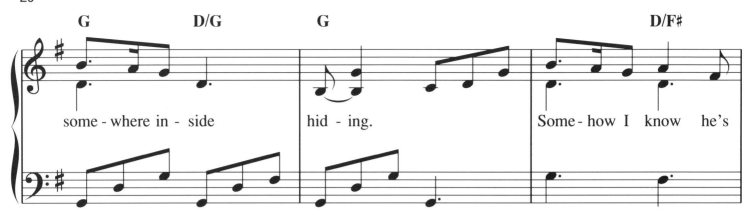

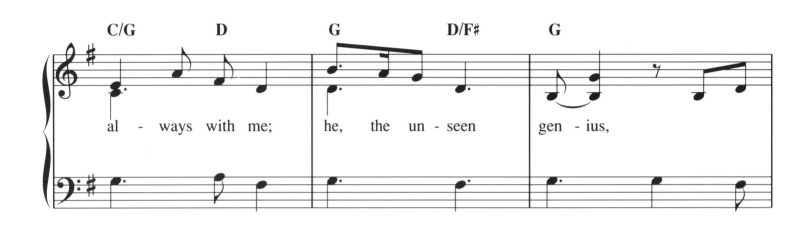

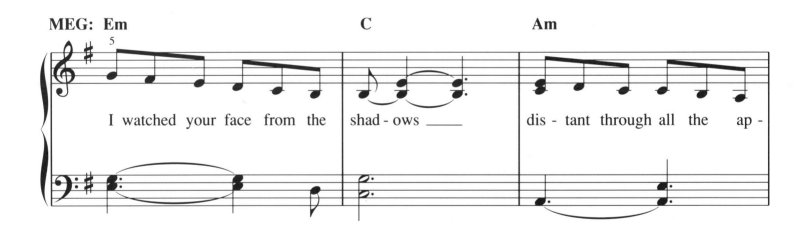

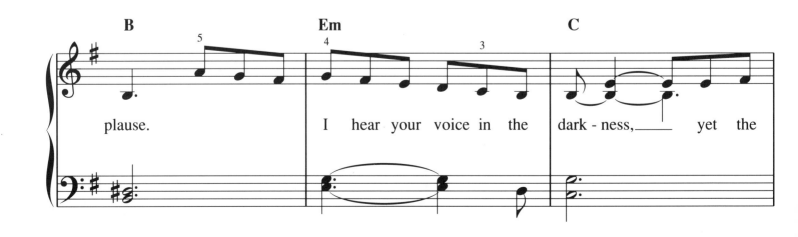

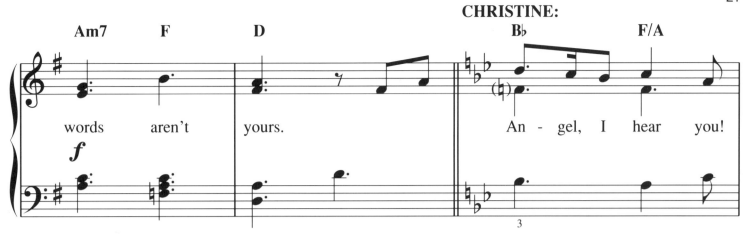

CHRISTINE:

words aren't yours. An - gel, I hear you!

Speak, I lis - ten. Stay by my side, guide me! _____

An - gel, my soul was weak; for - give me! En - ter at last,

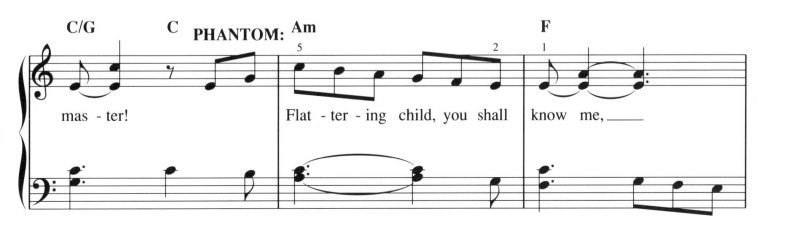

PHANTOM:

mas - ter! Flat - ter - ing child, you shall know me, _____

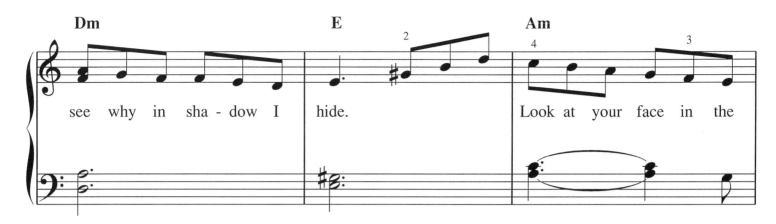

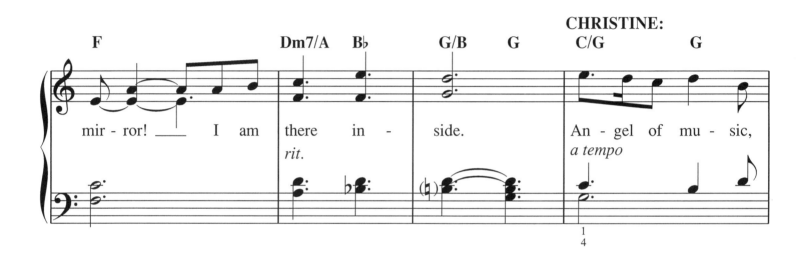

CHRISTINE:

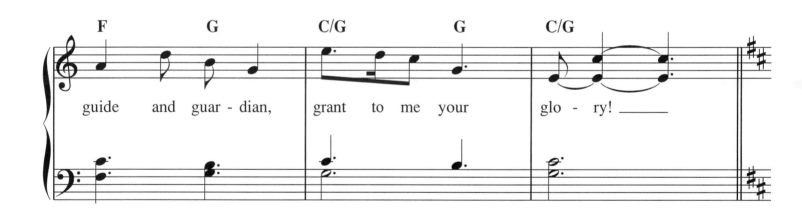

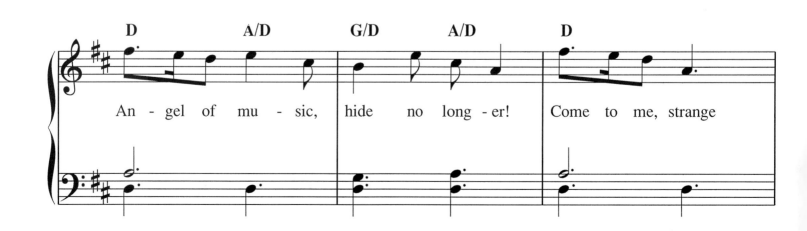

Moderately fast

an - gel! _____ I am your an - gel of mu - sic;

rit. *mf*

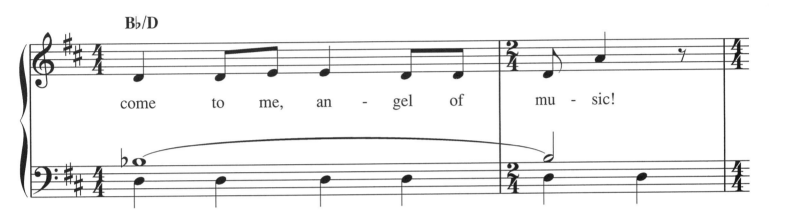

Bb/D

come to me, an - gel of mu - sic!

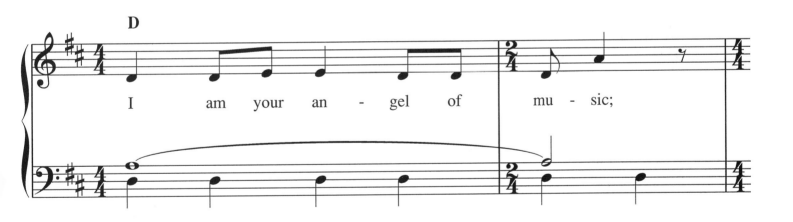

D

I am your an - gel of mu - sic;

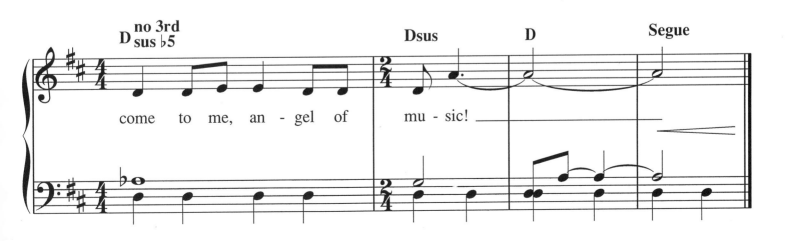

D sus b5 no 3rd   **Dsus**   **D**   **Segue**

come to me, an - gel of mu - sic! _____

THE PHANTOM OF THE OPERA

Lyrics by CHARLES HART,
RICHARD STILGOE and MIKE BATT
Music by ANDREW LLOYD WEBBER

Moderately fast

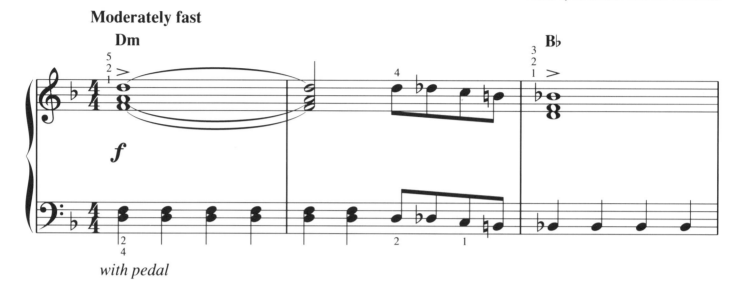

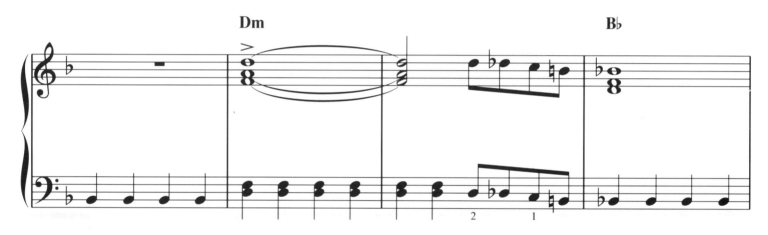

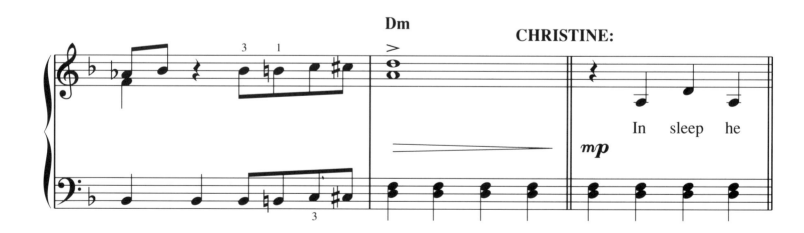

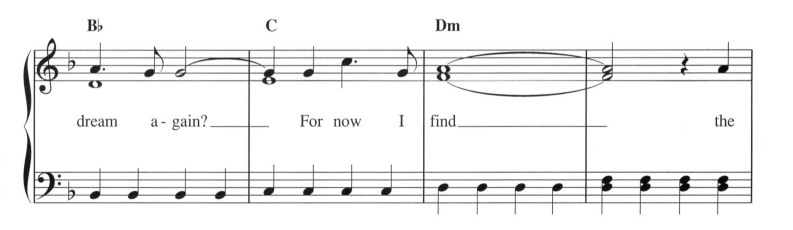

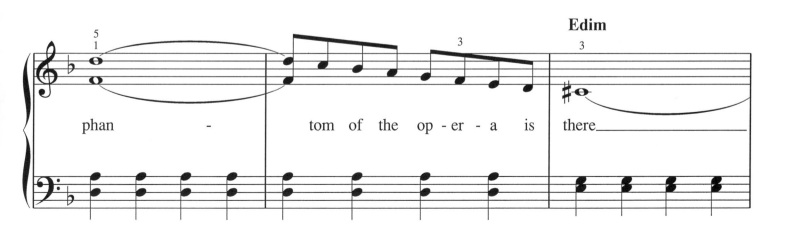

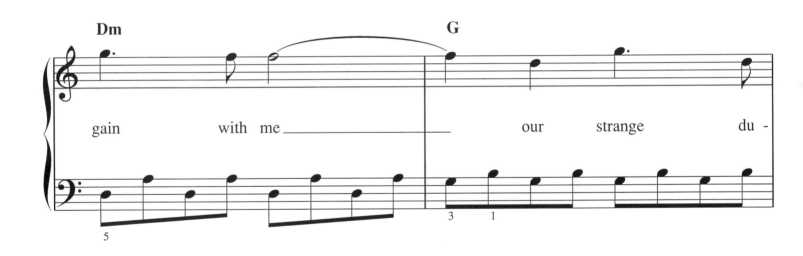

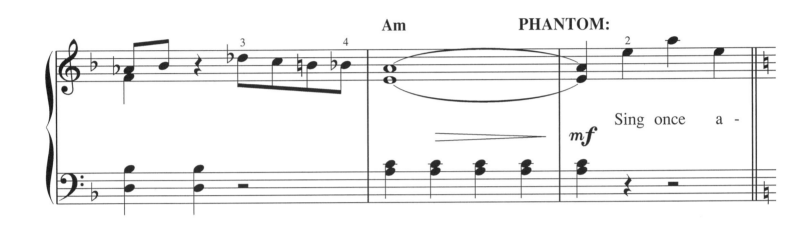

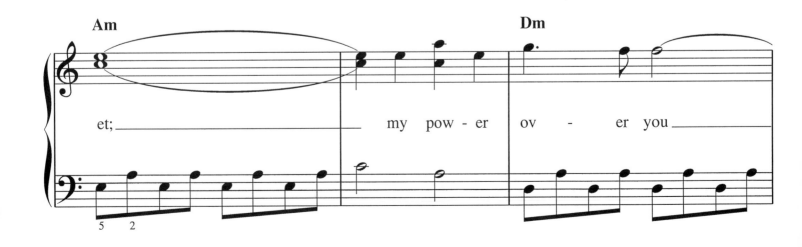

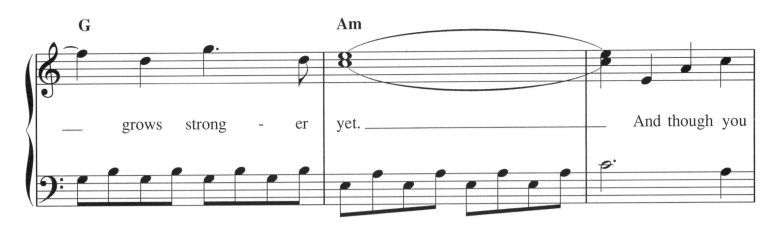

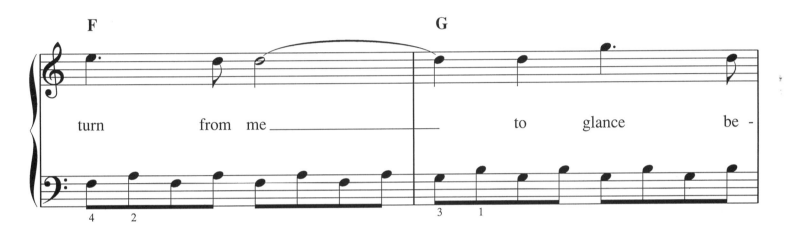

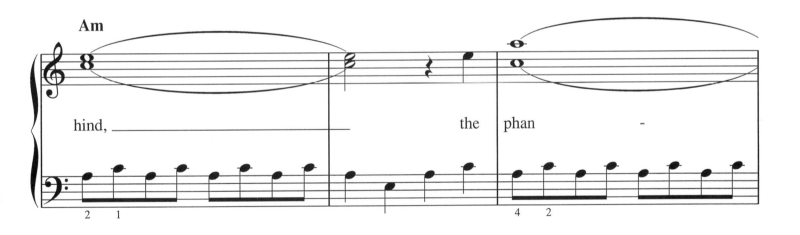

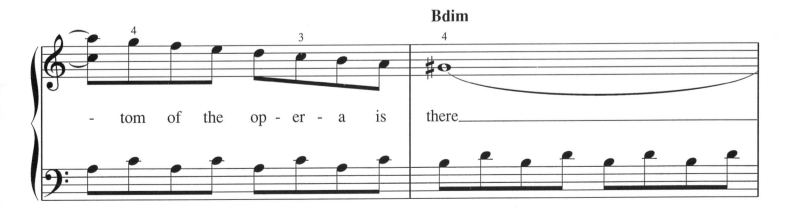

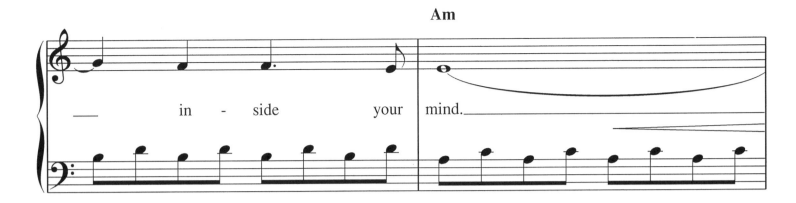

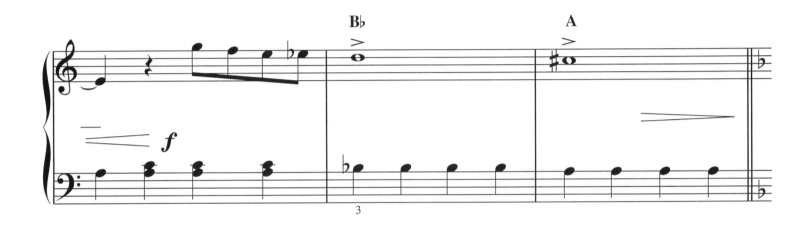

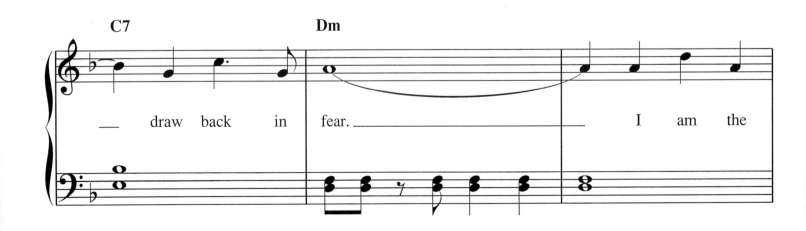

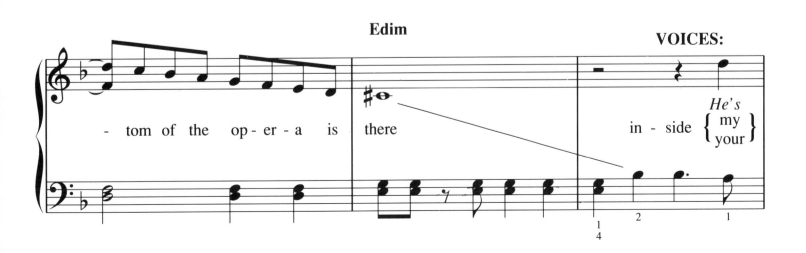

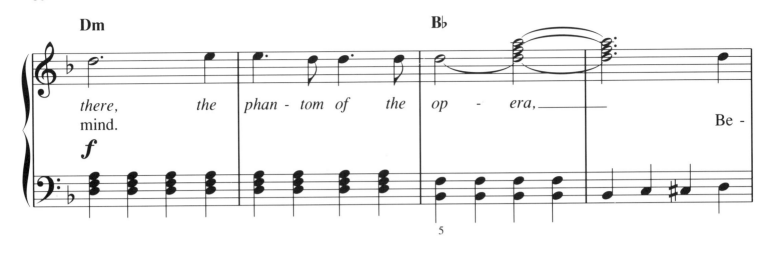

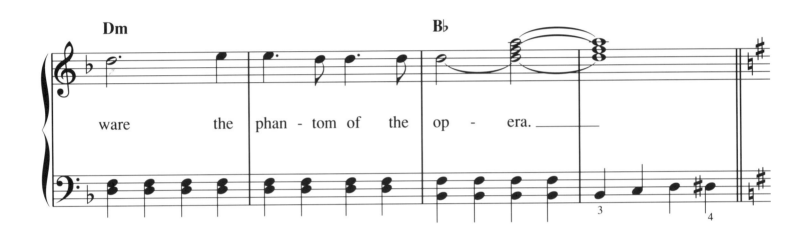

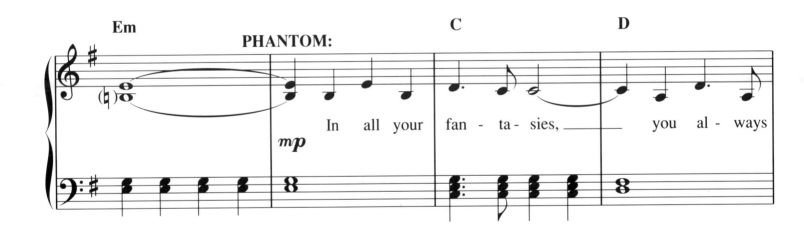

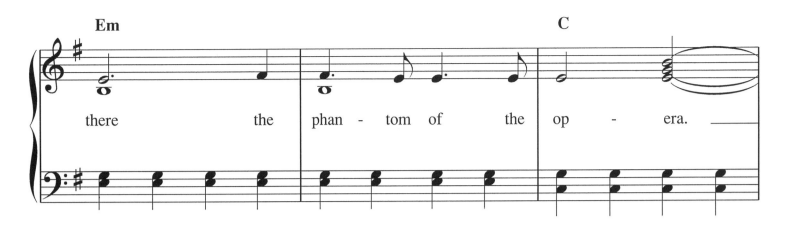

there the phan - tom of the op - era. _____

_____ Ah. _____

_____ *Sing, my angel, sing!* Ah! _____

PHANTOM:

CHRISTINE:

PHANTOM:

Sing for me!

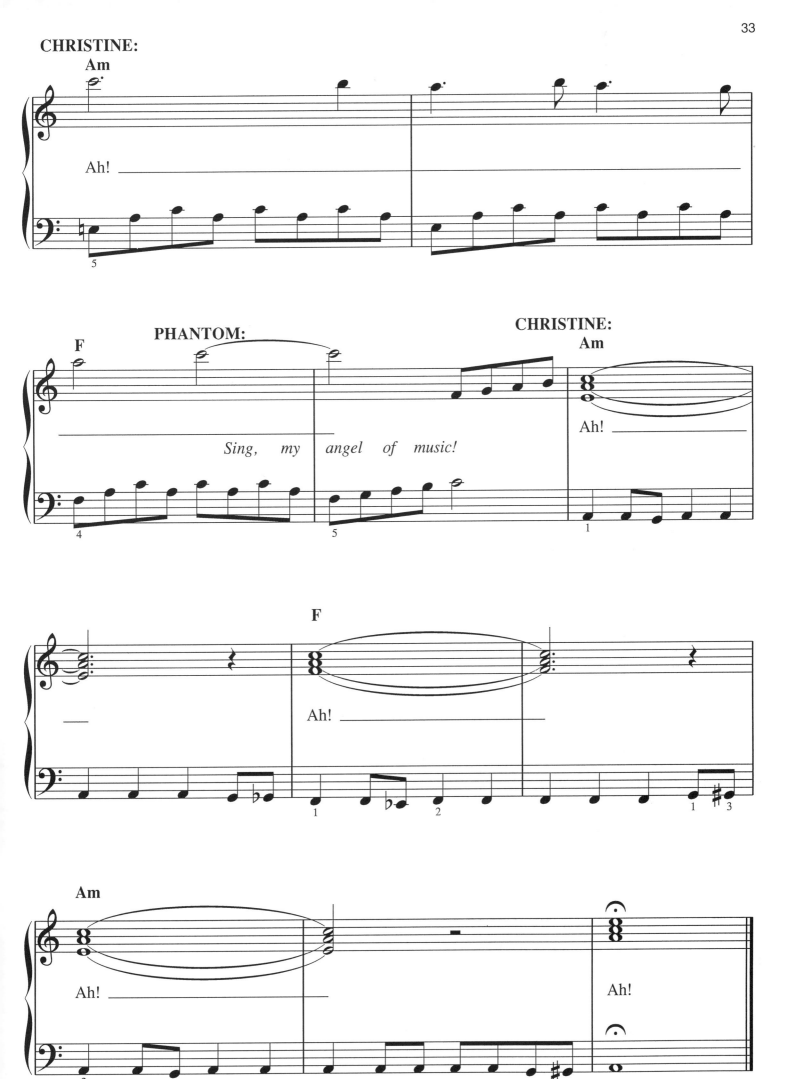

*Softly, deftly,
music shall caress you . . .
Hear it, feel it
secretly possess you . . .*

THE MUSIC OF THE NIGHT

Lyrics by CHARLES HART and RICHARD STILGOE
Music by ANDREW LLOYD WEBBER

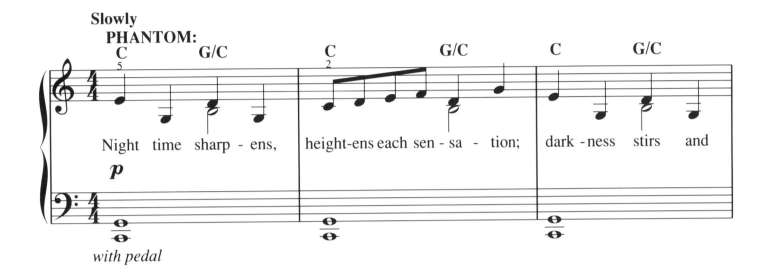

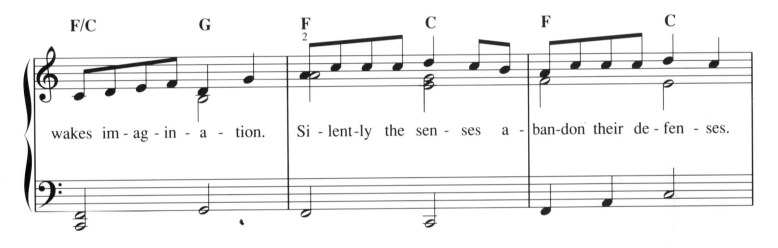

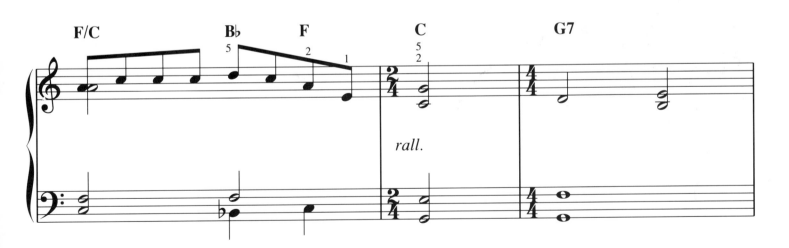

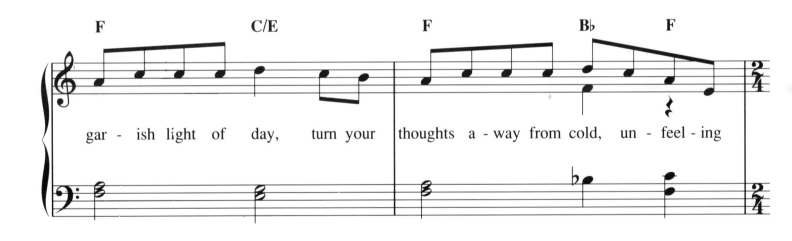

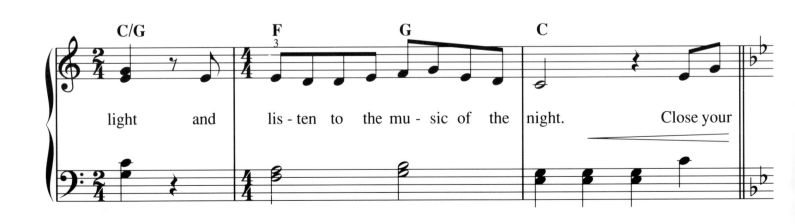

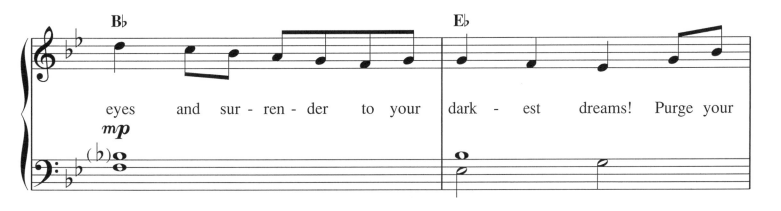

eyes and sur - ren - der to your dark - est dreams! Purge your

thoughts of the life you knew be - fore! Close your

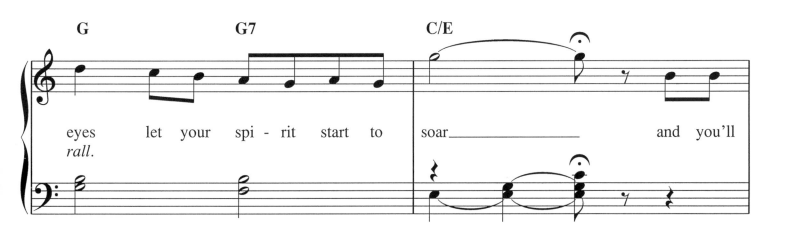

eyes let your spi - rit start to soar_____ and you'll

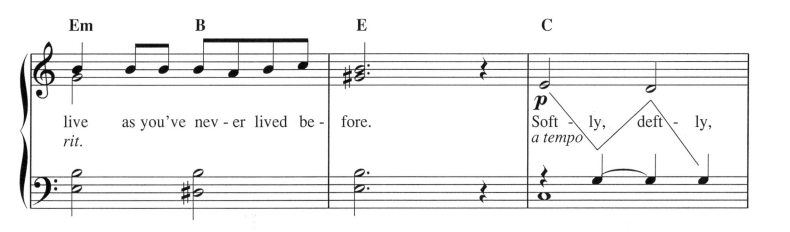

live as you've nev - er lived be - fore. Soft - ly, deft - ly,

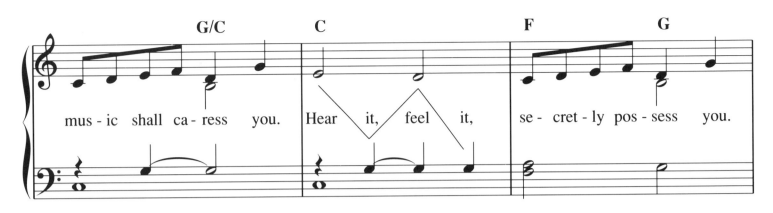

mus - ic shall ca - ress you. Hear it, feel it, se - cret - ly pos - sess you.

O - pen up your mind, let your fan - ta - sies un - wind in this

dark-ness which you know you can-not fight, the dark-ness of the mu - sic of the

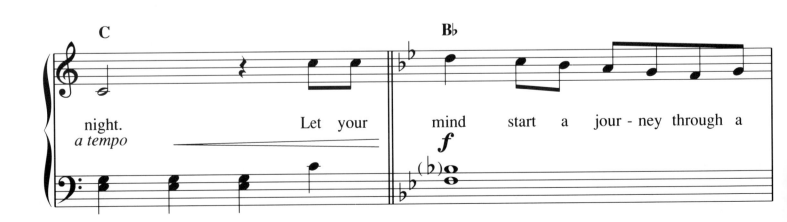

night. Let your mind start a jour - ney through a

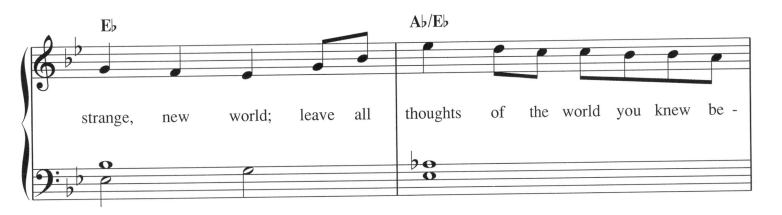

strange, new world; leave all thoughts of the world you knew be -

fore. Let your soul take you where you long to
rit.

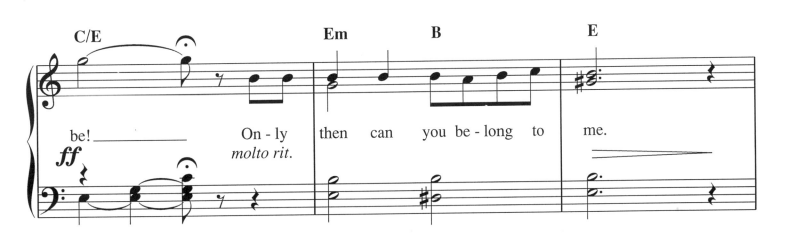

be! _____ On - ly then can you be - long to me.
molto rit.

ff

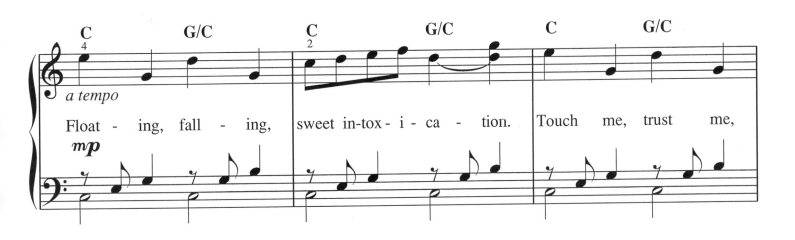

Float - ing, fall - ing, sweet in - tox - i - ca - tion. Touch me, trust me,
a tempo

mp

sa - vour each sen - sa - tion. Let the dream be - gin, let your

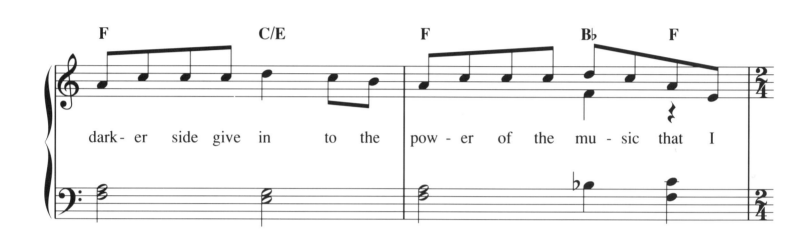

dark - er side give in to the pow - er of the mu - sic that I

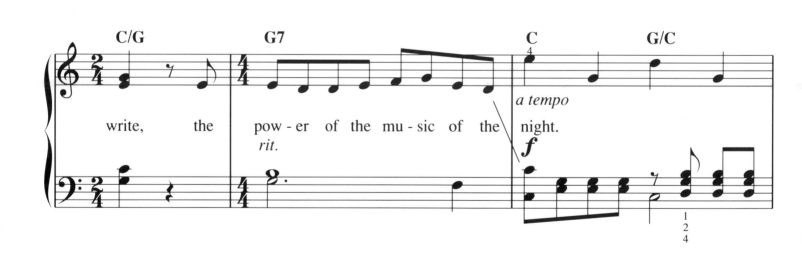

write, the pow - er of the mu - sic of the night.

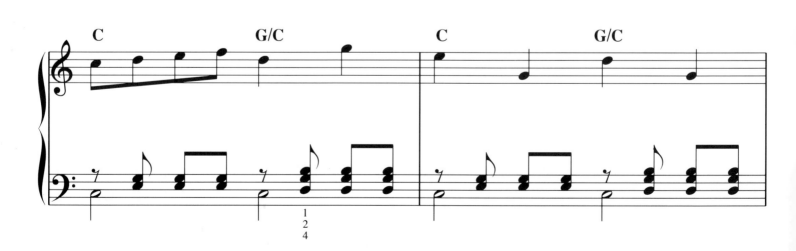

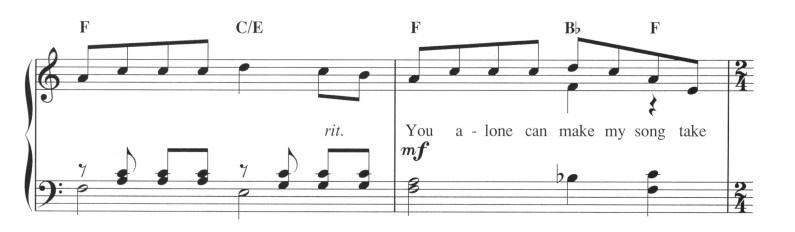

rit.

You a - lone can make my song take

flight, help me make the mu - sic of the night.

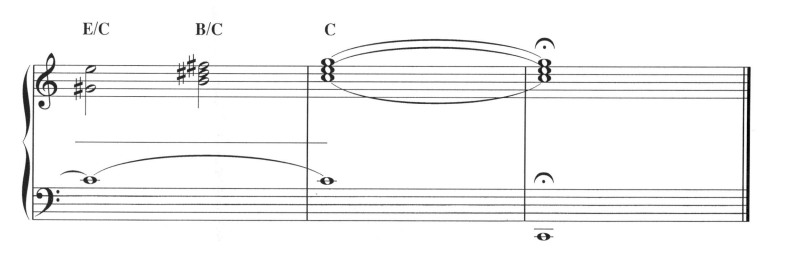

PRIMA DONNA

bow-wow

Lyrics by CHARLES HART and RICHARD STILGOE
Music by ANDREW LLOYD WEBBER

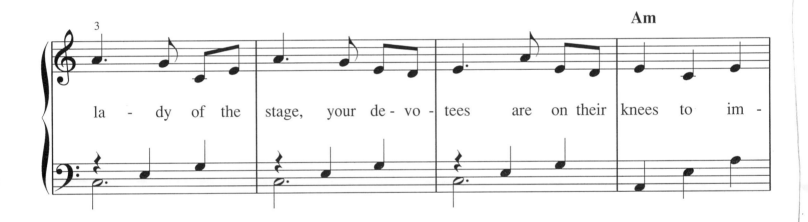

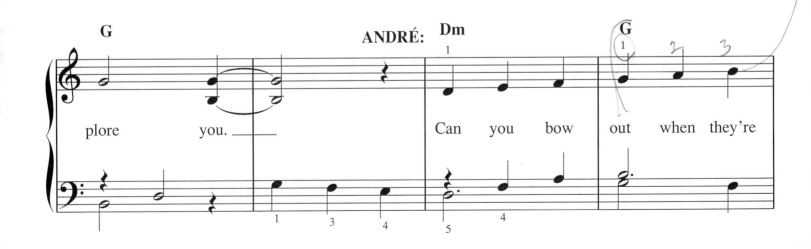

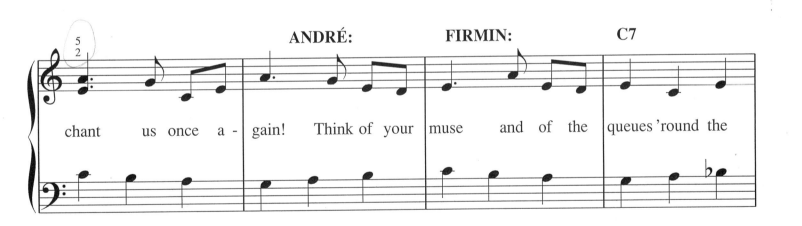

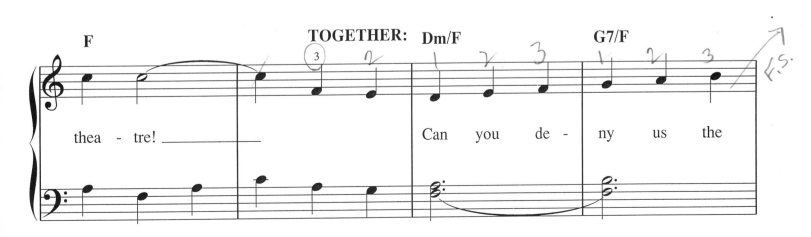

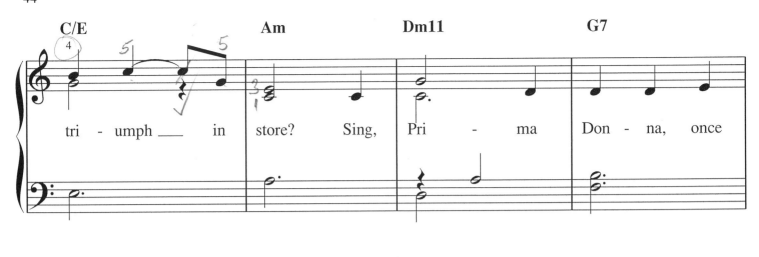

tri - umph ___ in store? Sing, Pri - ma Don - na, once

C   **C7**   **CARLOTTA:**   **F**

more!   Pri - ma Don - na, your

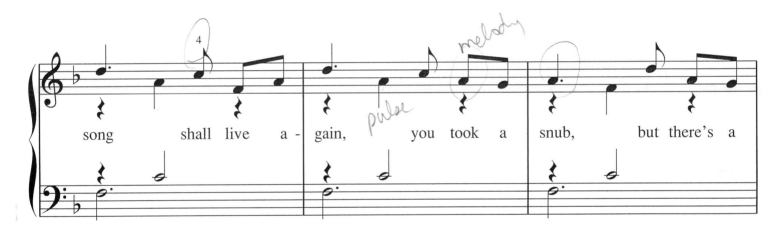

song shall live a - gain, you took a snub, but there's a

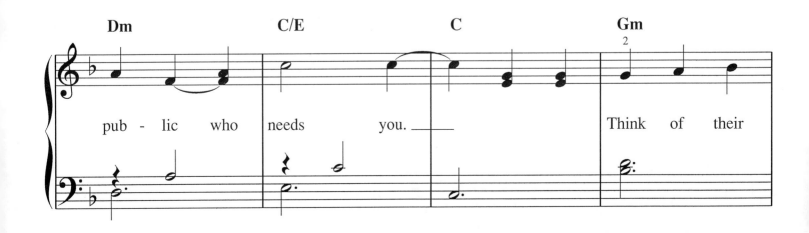

Dm   **C/E**   **C**   **Gm**

pub - lic who needs you. ___ Think of their

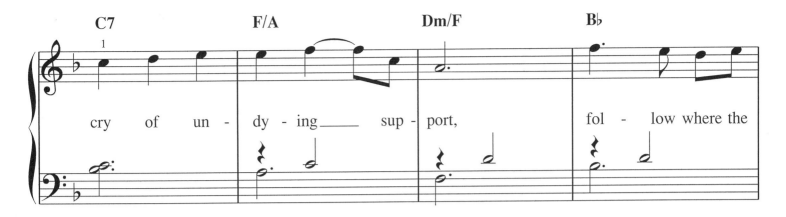

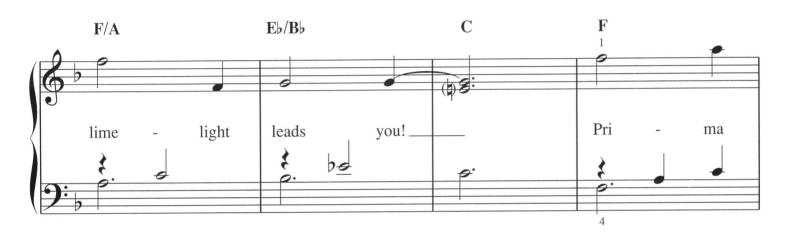

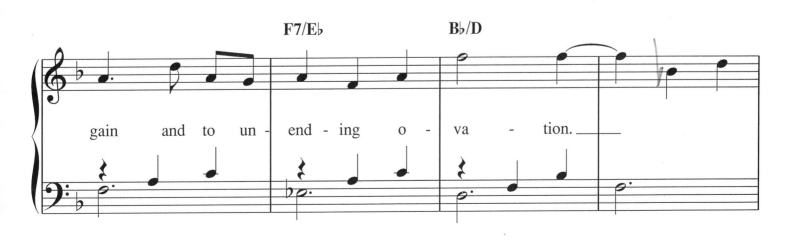

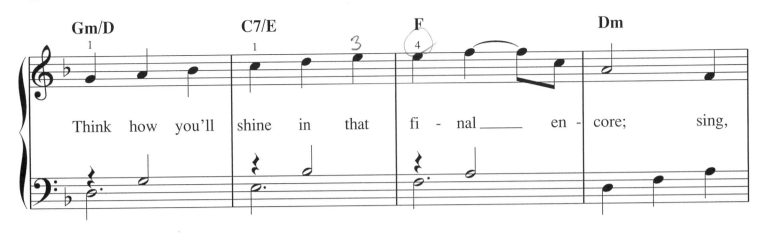

Think how you'll shine in that fi - nal _____ en - core; sing,

Pri - ma Don - na, once more!

ANDRÉ and FIRMIN:

Who'd be - lieve a di - va hap - py to re - lieve a cho - rus girl who's gone and

slept with the pa - tron? __ Raoul and the soub - rette en - twined in love's du - et; al -

though he may de-mur he must have been with her. You'd nev-er get a-way with

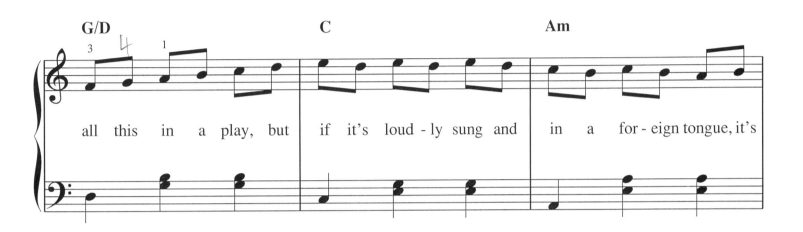

all this in a play, but if it's loud-ly sung and in a for-eign tongue, it's

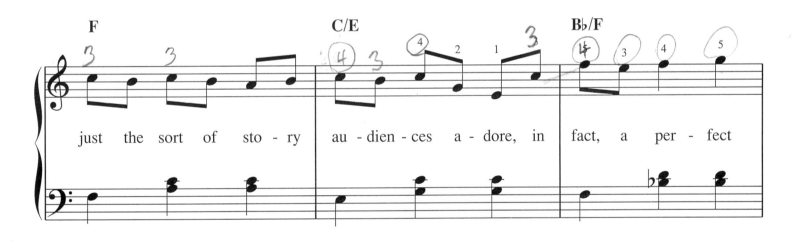

just the sort of sto-ry au-dien-ces a-dore, in fact, a per-fect

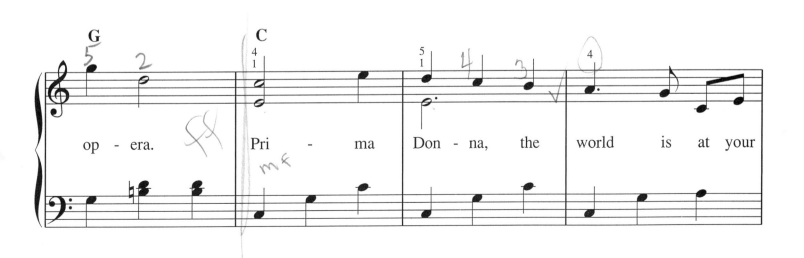

op-era. Pri-ma Don-na, the world is at your

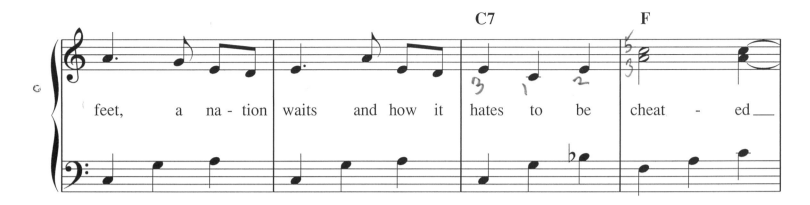

feet, a na - tion waits and how it hates to be cheat - ed___

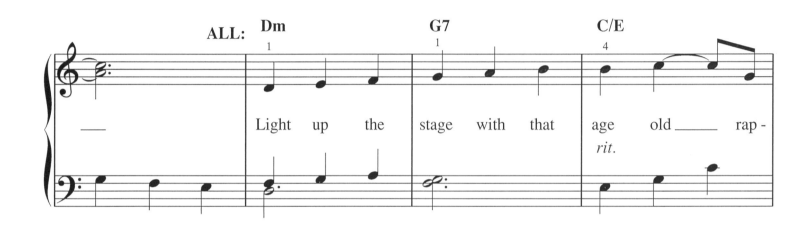

ALL: ___ Light up the stage with that age old___ rap -
rit.

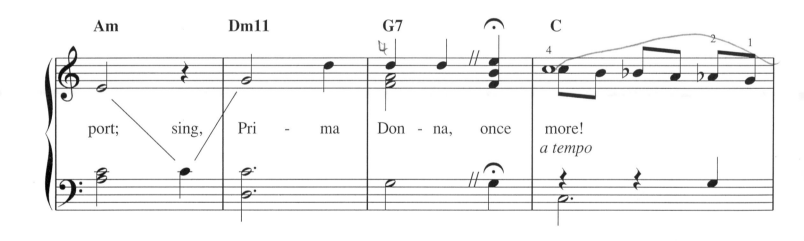

port; sing, Pri - ma Don - na, once more!
a tempo

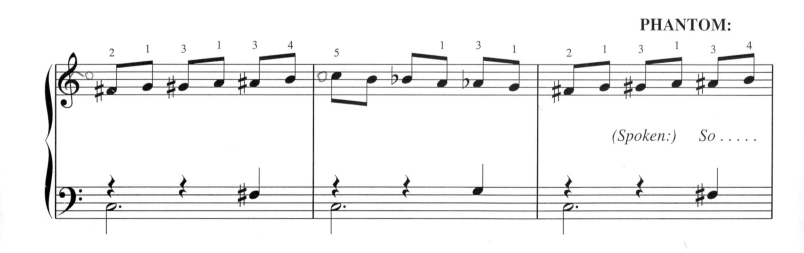

PHANTOM:

(Spoken:) So . . . . .

It is to be a war between us? If these

demands are not met a disaster beyond your imagination

ALL: G

will occur. Once

C

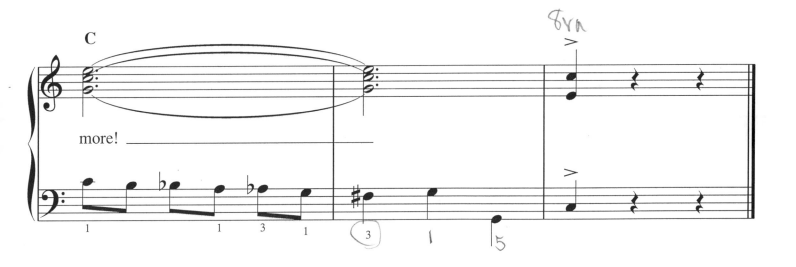

more!

ALL I ASK OF YOU

Lyrics by CHARLES HART and RICHARD STILGOE
Music by ANDREW LLOYD WEBBER

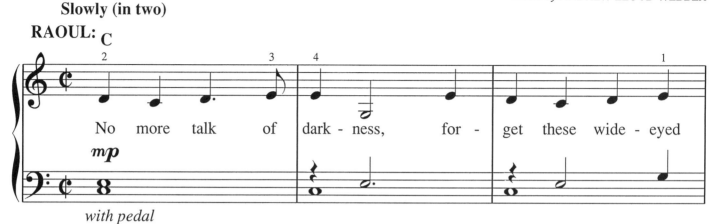

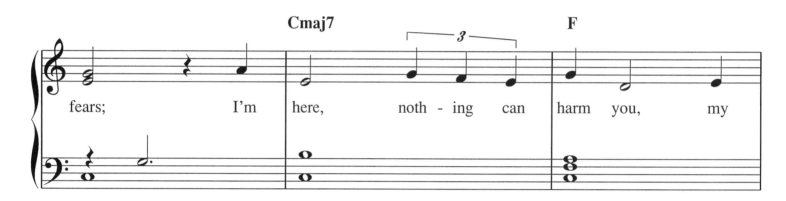

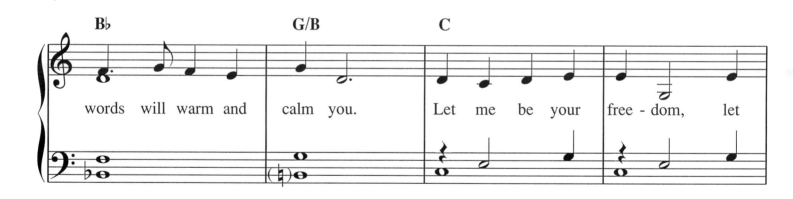

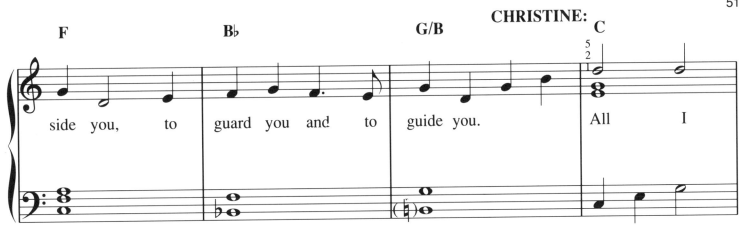

CHRISTINE:

side you,   to   guard you and   to   guide you.   All   I

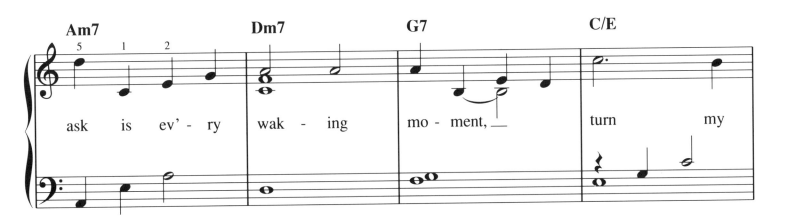

ask   is   ev'- ry   wak - ing   mo - ment, ___   turn   my

head   with   talk   of   sum - mer - time.

Say   you   need me with you   now   and   al - ways; ___

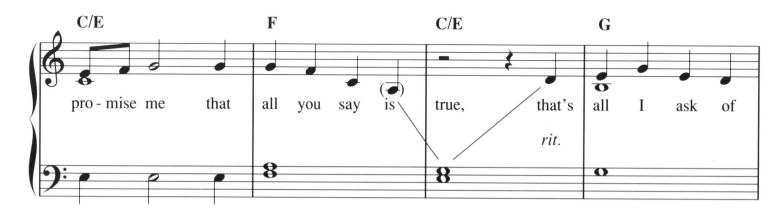

C/E   **F**   **C/E**   **G**

pro - mise me that all you say is true, that's all I ask of

rit.

RAOUL:

C

mf
Let me be your shel - ter, let me be your light; you're
you.

a tempo

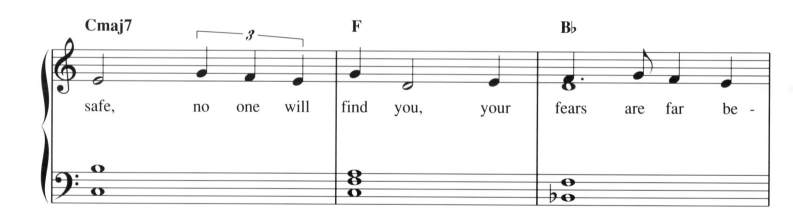

Cmaj7   **F**   **B♭**

safe, no one will find you, your fears are far be -

CHRISTINE:

G/B   **C**

hind you. All I want is free - dom, a world with no more

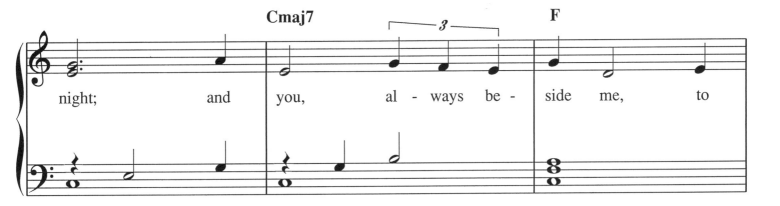

night;   and   you,   al - ways be -   side me,   to

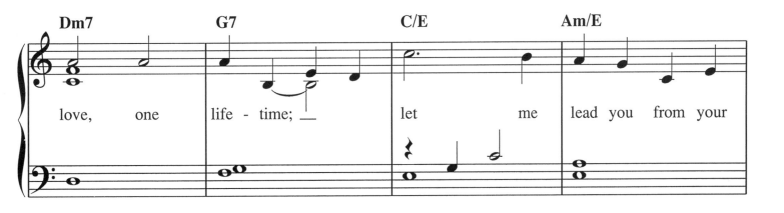

hold   me and   to   hide   me.   Then   say   you'll   share   with   me   one

love,   one   life - time; ___   let   me   lead   you   from your

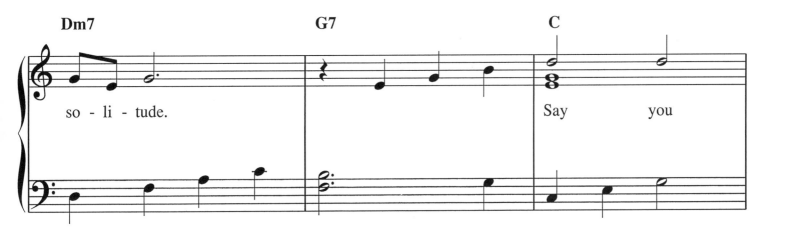

so - li - tude.   Say   you

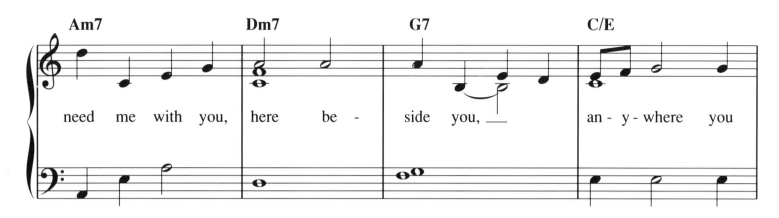

need me with you, here be - side you, ___ an-y-where you

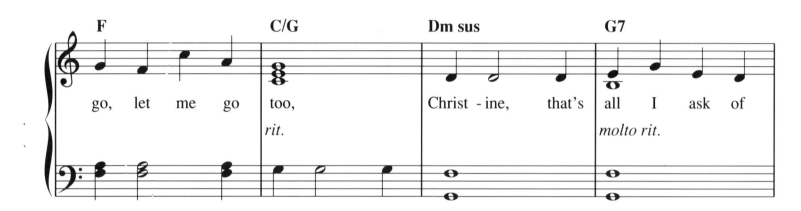

go, let me go too, Christ - ine, that's all I ask of
rit. *molto rit.*

CHRISTINE:

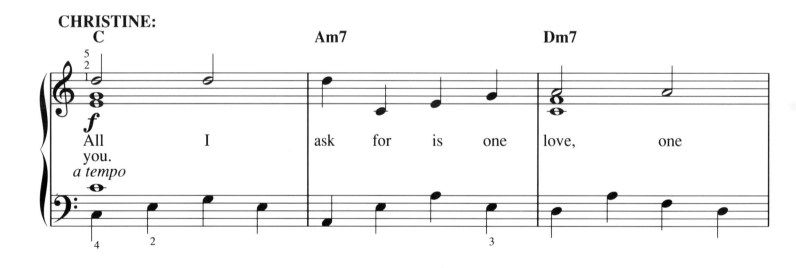

All I ask for is one love, one
you.
a tempo

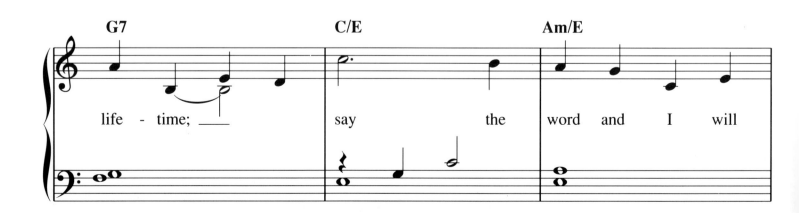

life - time; ___ say the word and I will

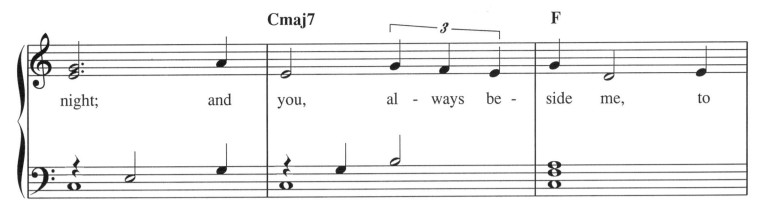

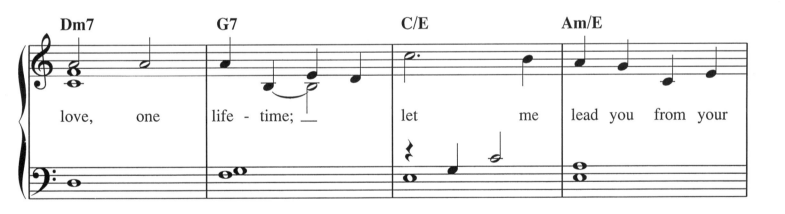

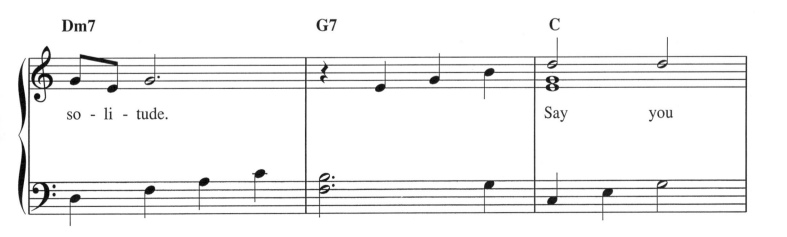

54

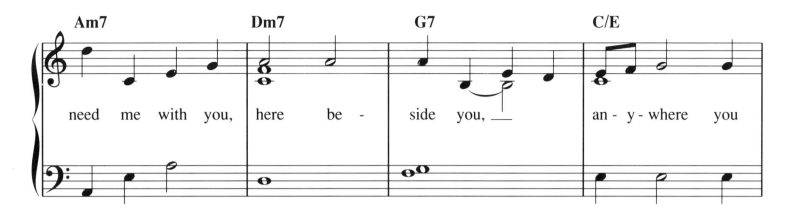

need me with you, here be - side you, ___ an - y - where you

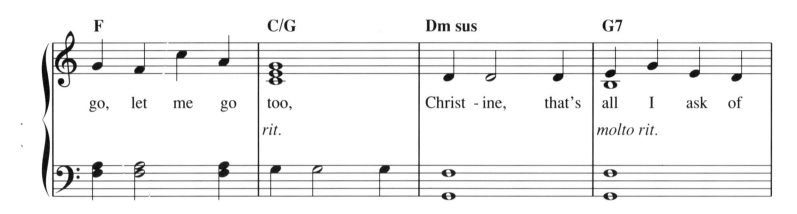

go, let me go too, Christ - ine, that's all I ask of

CHRISTINE:

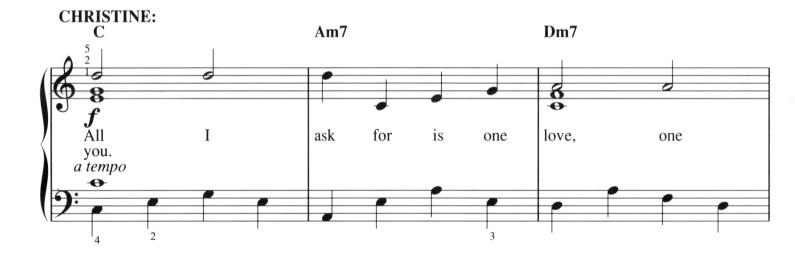

All I ask for is one love, one

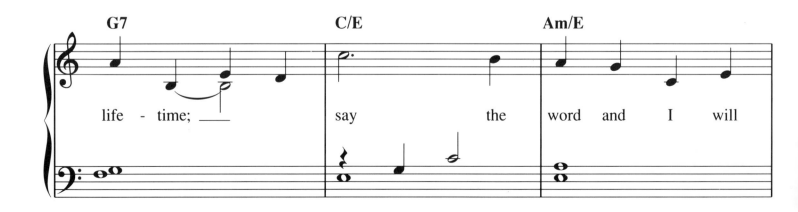

life - time; ___ say the word and I will

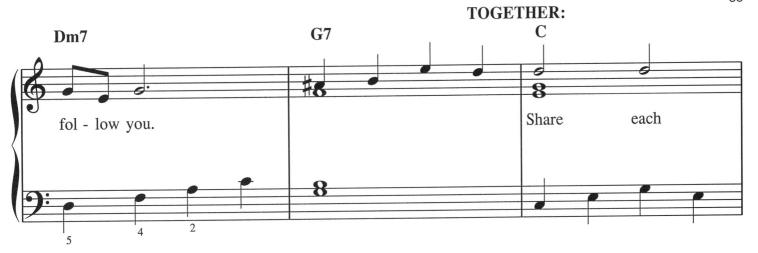

TOGETHER:

fol - low you.   Share   each

day   with   me,   each   night,   each   morn - ing. ____

Slower

An - y - where   you   go,   let   me   go   too;

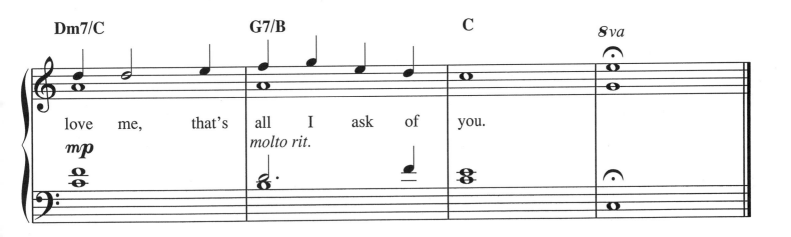

love   me,   that's   all   I   ask   of   you.

*What I once used to dream
I now dread . . .
if he finds me, it won't
ever end . . .*

We've passed the point
of no return . . .

MASQUERADE

Lyrics by CHARLES HART and RICHARD STILGOE
Music by ANDREW LLOYD WEBBER

Slowly (in two)

CHORUS:

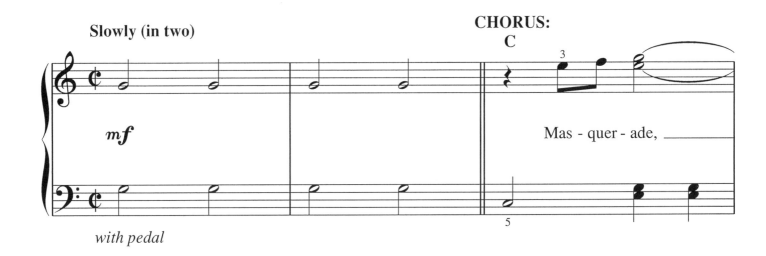

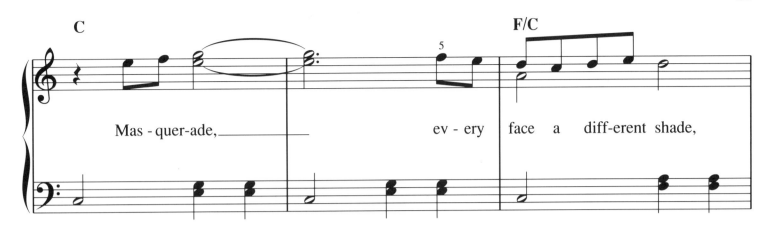

Mas - quer-ade,_____ ev - ery face a diff-erent shade,

mas - quer-ade,_____ look a - round there's an - oth – er mask be -

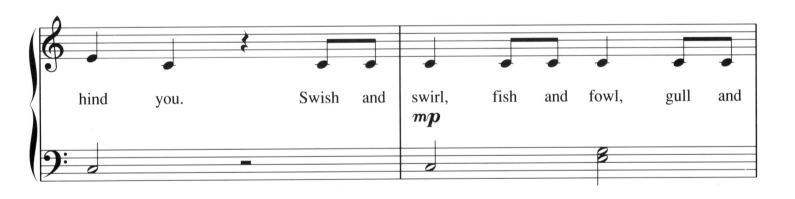

hind you. Swish and swirl, fish and fowl, gull and

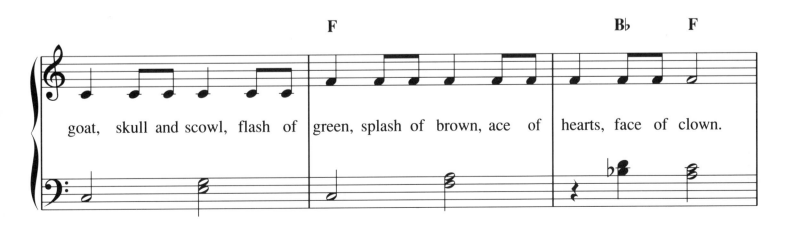

goat, skull and scowl, flash of green, splash of brown, ace of hearts, face of clown.

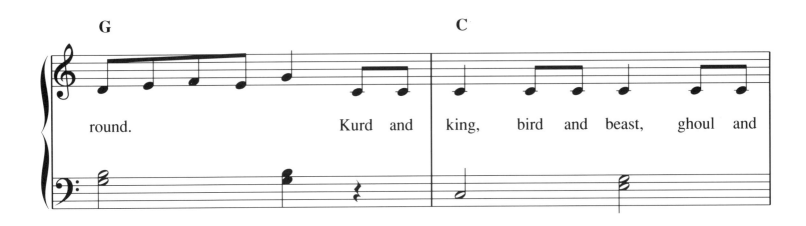

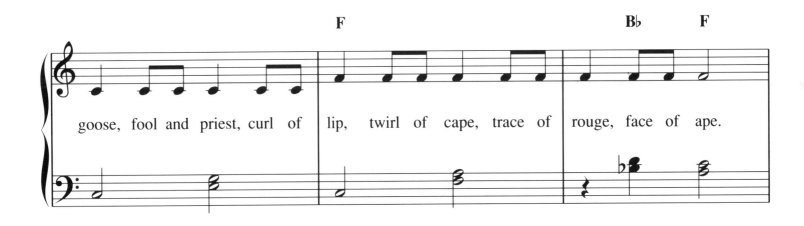

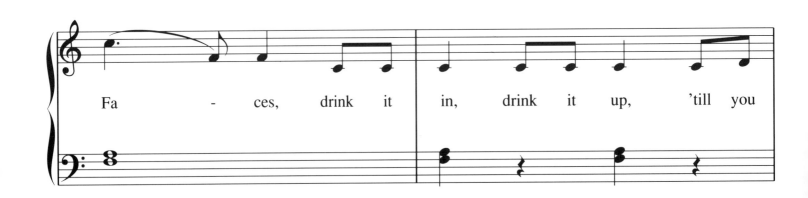

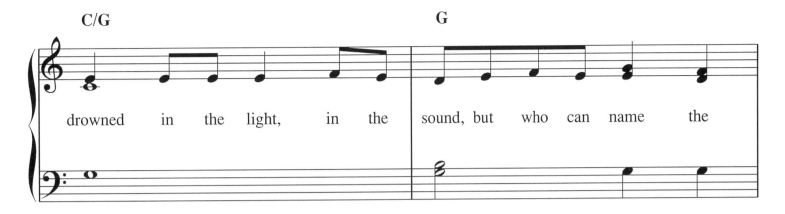

drowned in the light, in the sound, but who can name the

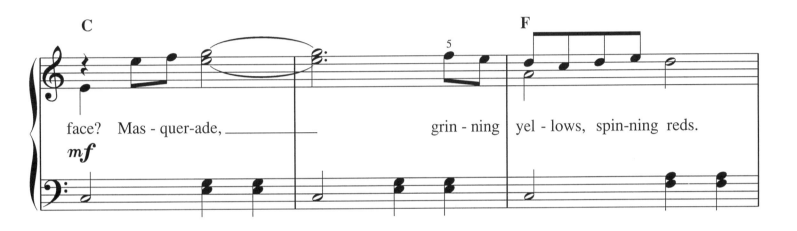

face? Mas-quer-ade, _____ grin-ning yel-lows, spin-ning reds.

mf

Mas-quer-ade, _____ take your fill, let the spec-ta-cle as-

tound you, Mas-quer-ade, _____ burn-ing

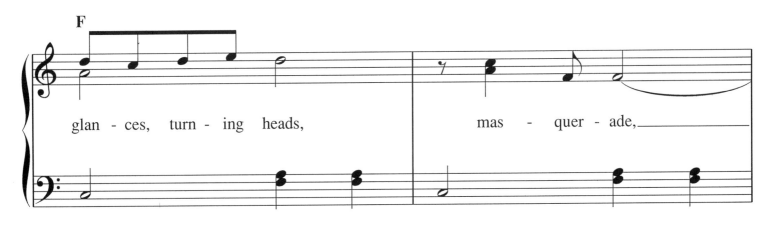

glan - ces, turn - ing heads,   mas - quer - ade,___

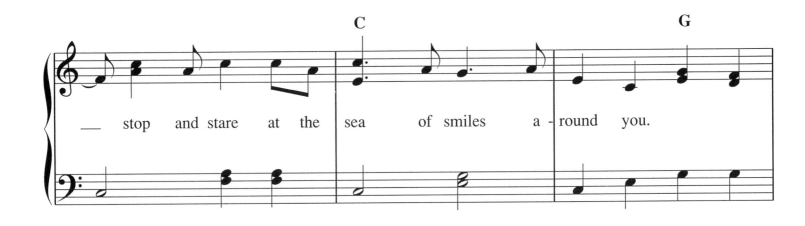

___ stop and stare at the sea of smiles a - round you.

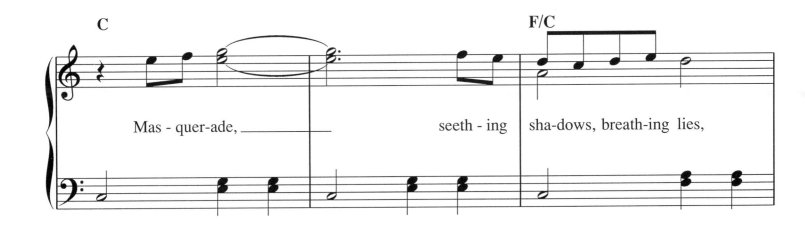

Mas - quer-ade,_____ seeth - ing sha-dows, breath-ing lies,

mas - quer-ade _____ you can fool an - y friend who ev - er

knew you. Mas - quer - ade, _____ leer - ing

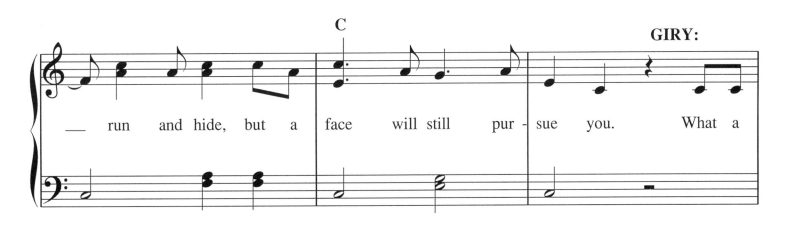

sa - tyrs, peer - ing eyes, mas - quer - ade, _____

___ run and hide, but a face will still pur - sue you. What a

MEG, ANDRÉ: **FIRMIN:**

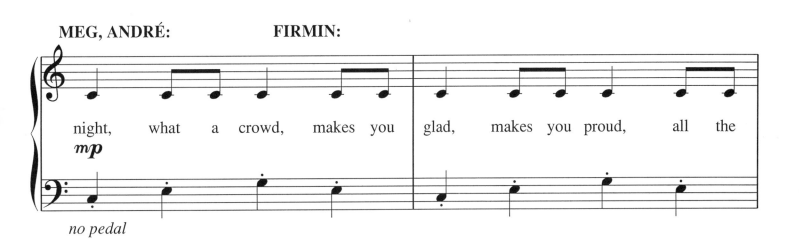

night, what a crowd, makes you glad, makes you proud, all the

no pedal

F

crème de-la crème watch-ing us, watch-ing them, six _____ months of re-

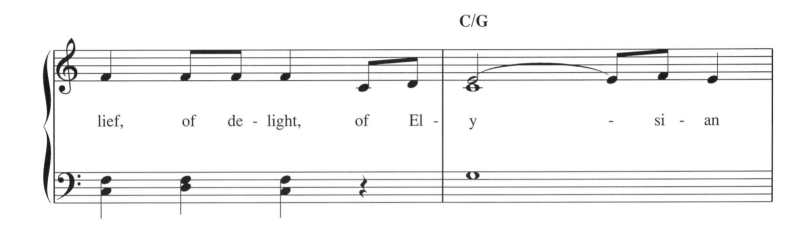

C/G

lief, of de - light, of El - y - si - an

G   **C**   **PIANGI:**   **GIRY:**

peace. No more notes, no more ghost, here's a

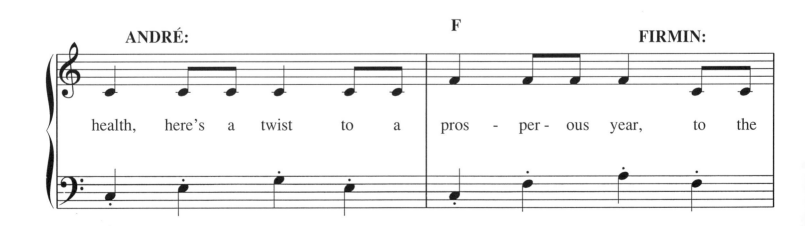

ANDRÉ: **F**   **FIRMIN:**

health, here's a twist to a pros - per - ous year, to the

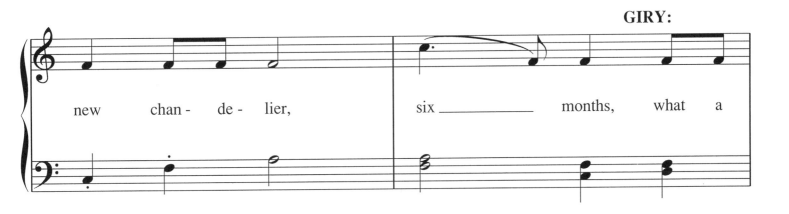

GIRY:

new chan - de - lier, six _____ months, what a

MEG:

FIRMIN
and
ANDRÉ:

C/G

joy, what a change, what a bless - ed re -

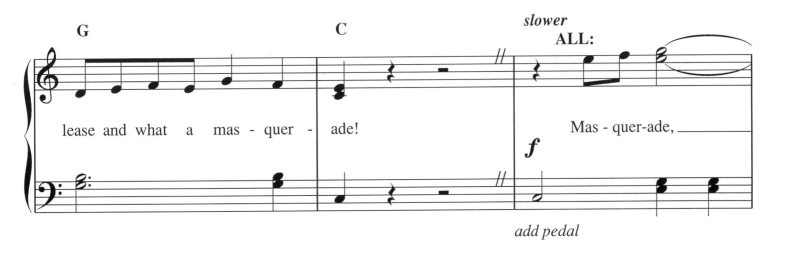

G

C

slower

ALL:

lease and what a mas - quer - ade! Mas - quer-ade, _____

add pedal

F/C

burn - ing glan-ces, turn - ing heads, Mas - quer - ade, _____

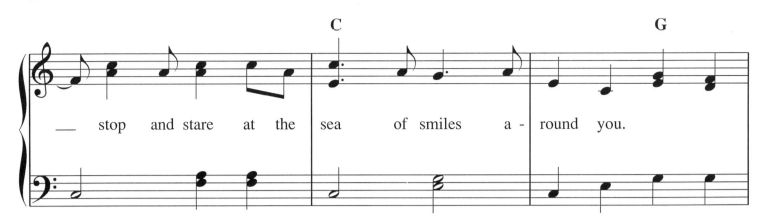

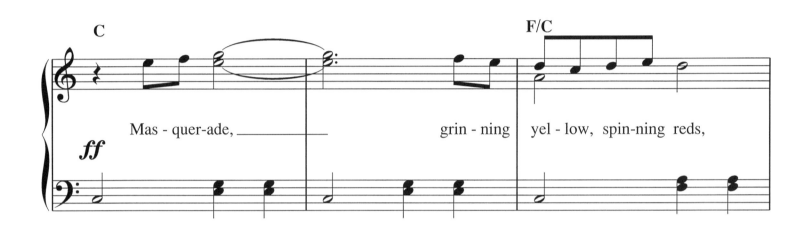

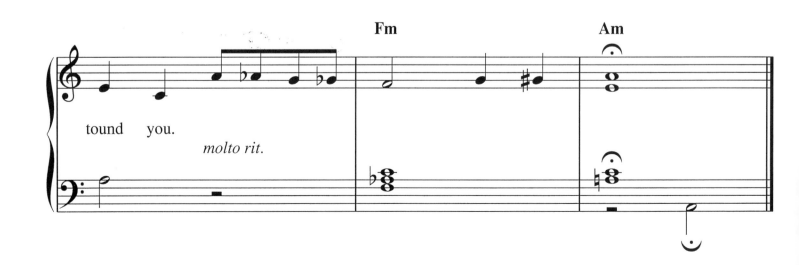

WISHING YOU WERE SOMEHOW HERE AGAIN

Lyrics by CHARLES HART and RICHARD STILGOE
Music by ANDREW LLOYD WEBBER

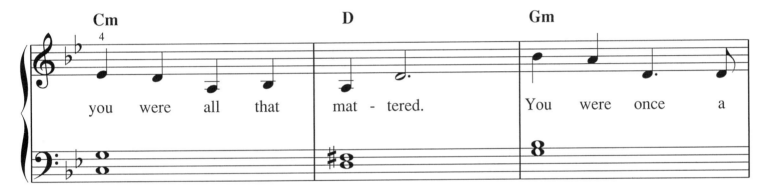

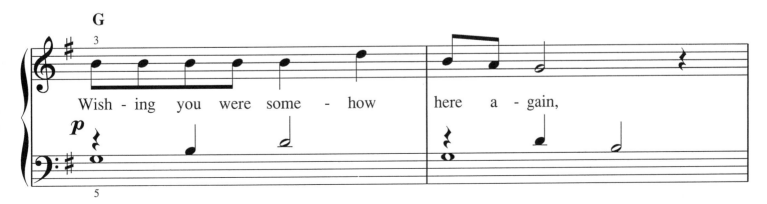

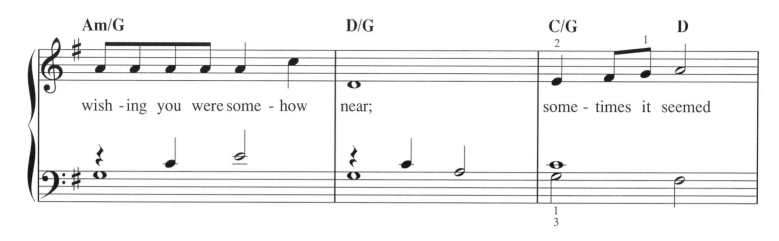

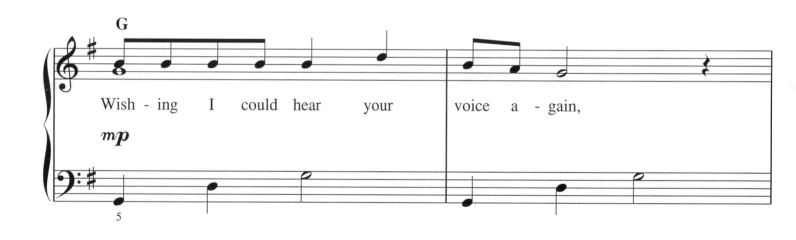

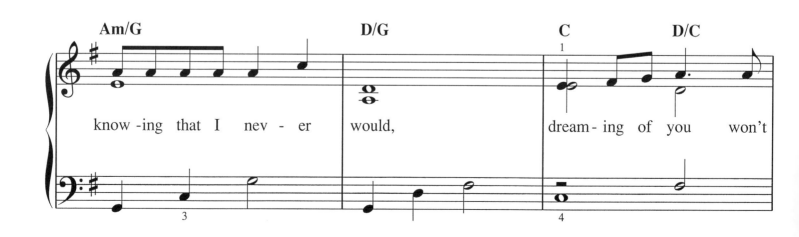

help me to do all that you dreamed I could.

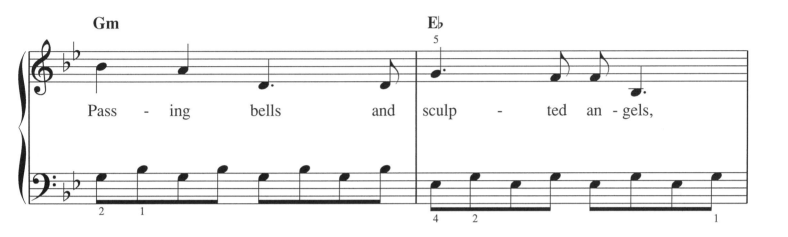

Pass - ing bells and sculp - ted an - gels,

cold and mon - u - men - tal, seem for you the

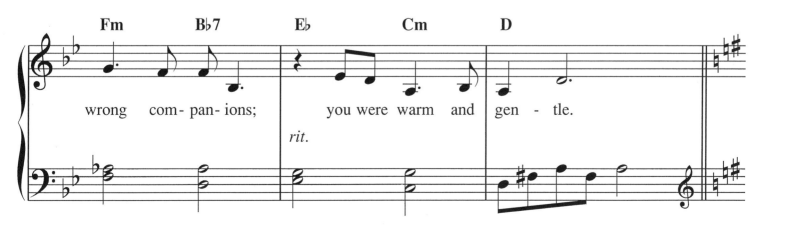

wrong com - pan - ions; you were warm and gen - tle.

rit.

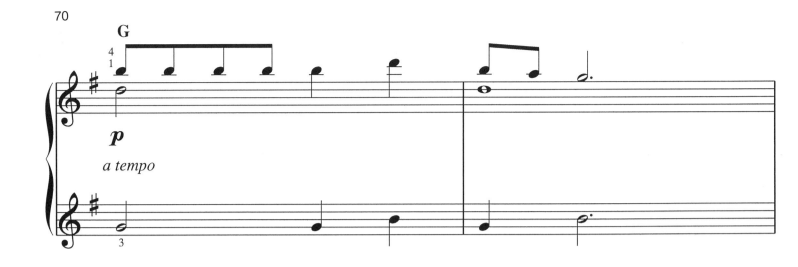

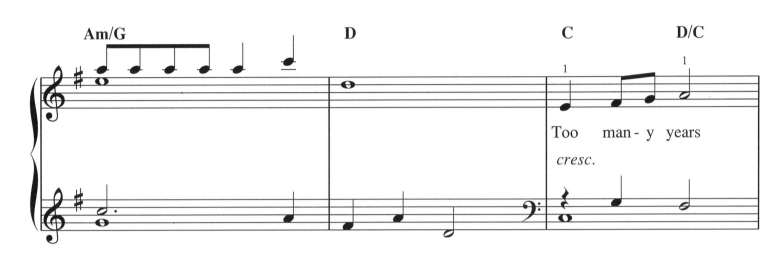

Too man - y years

cresc.

fight - ing back tears, why can't the past just die?

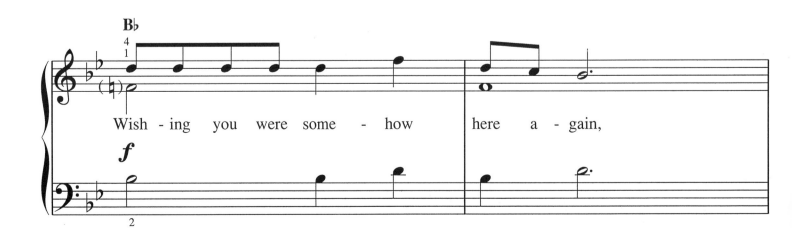

Wish - ing you were some - how here a - gain,

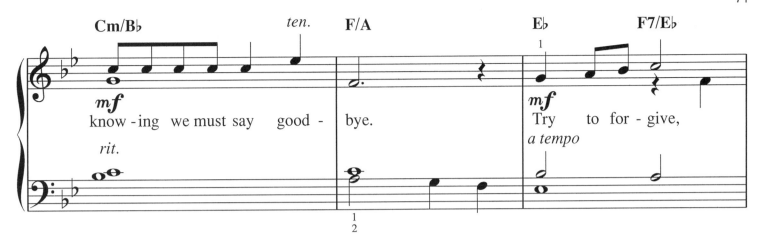

THE POINT OF NO RETURN

Lyrics by CHARLES HART and RICHARD STILGOE
Music by ANDREW LLOYD WEBBER

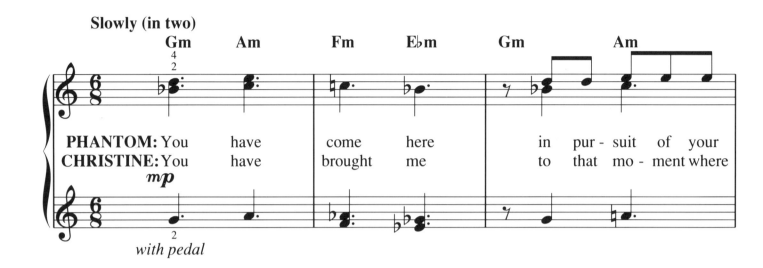

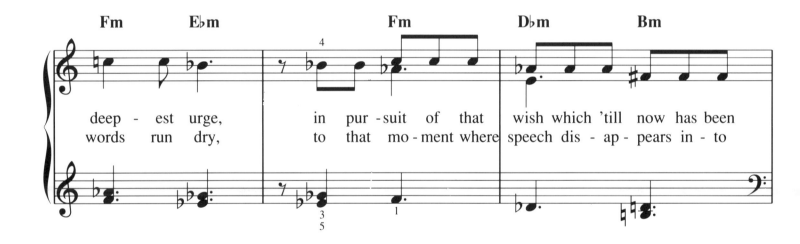

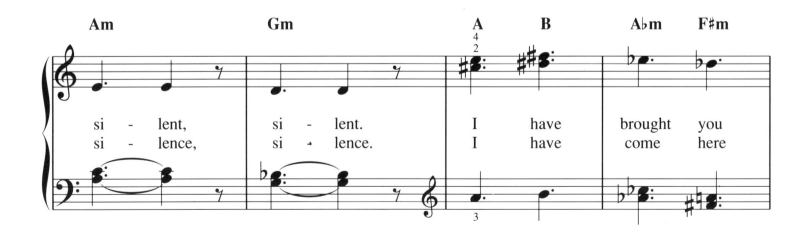

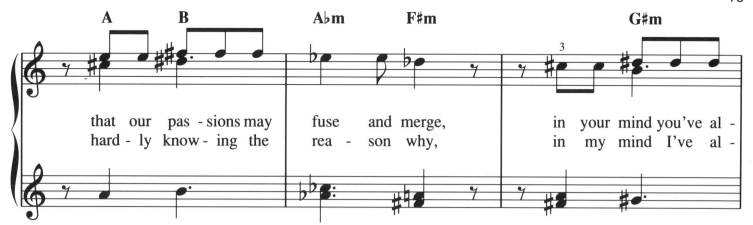

that our pas - sions may / fuse and merge, / in your mind you've al -
hard - ly know - ing the / rea - son why, / in my mind I've al -

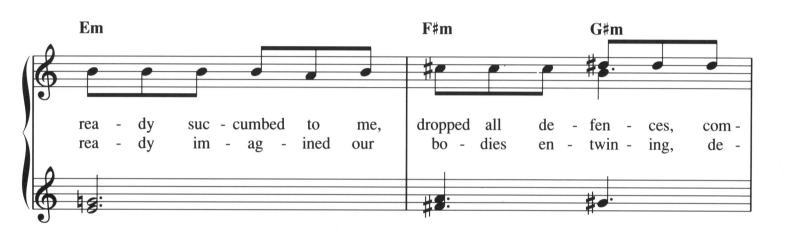

rea - dy suc - cumbed to me, / dropped all de - fen - ces, com -
rea - dy im - ag - ined our / bo - dies en - twin - ing, de -

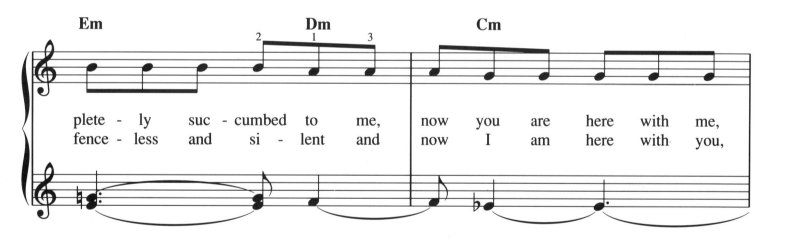

plete - ly suc - cumbed to me, / now you are here with me,
fence - less and si - lent and / now I am here with you,

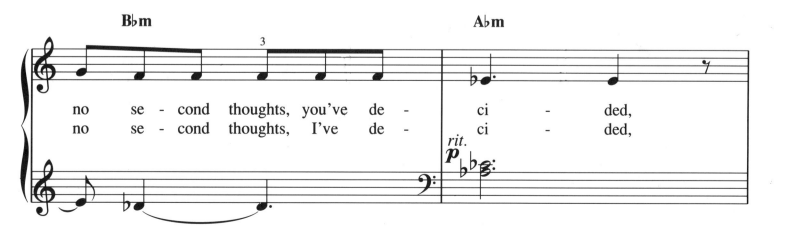

no se - cond thoughts, you've de - ci - ded,
no se - cond thoughts, I've de - ci - ded,

rit.
p

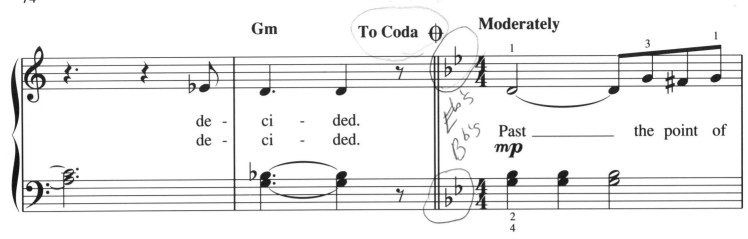

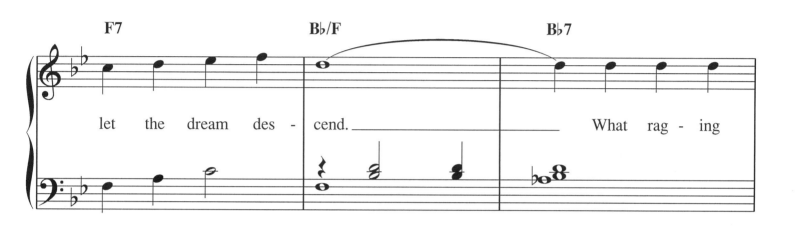

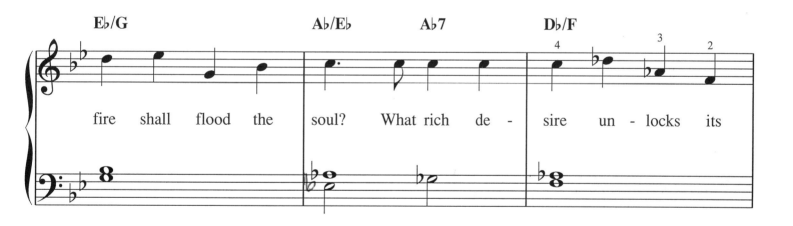

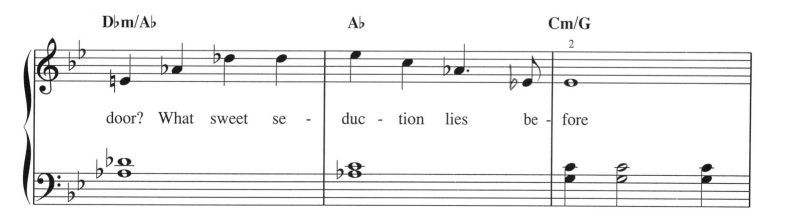

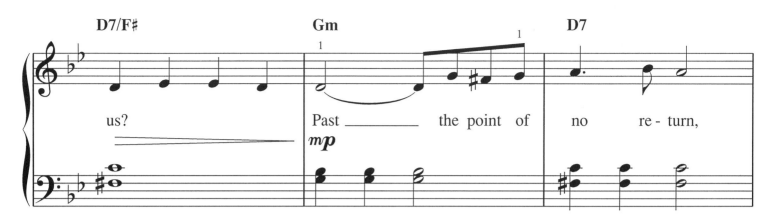

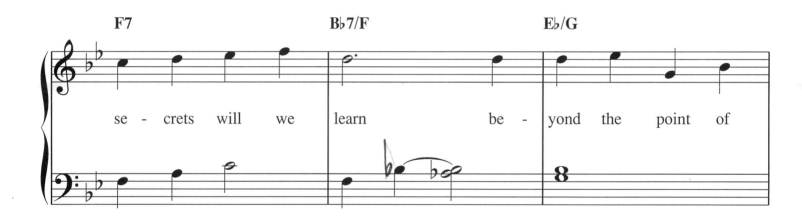

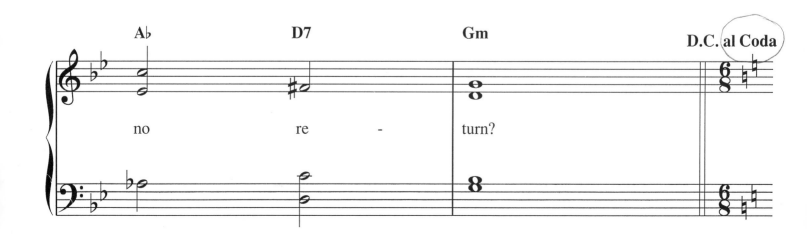

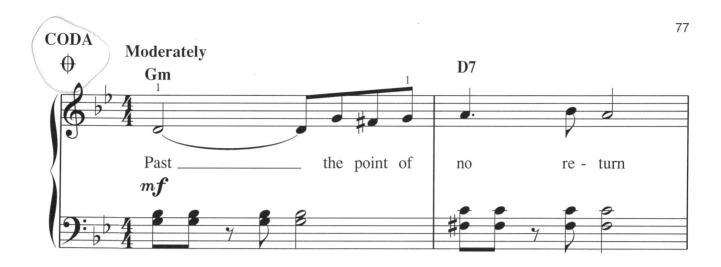

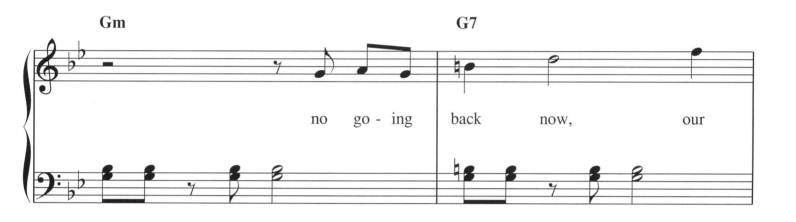

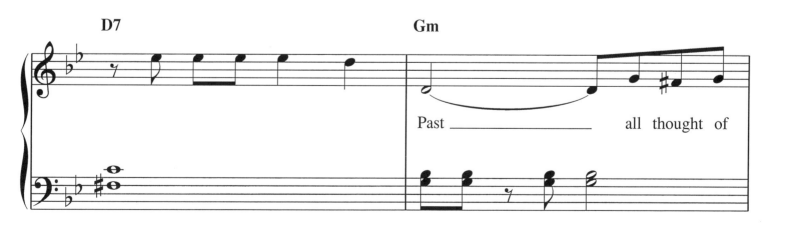

78

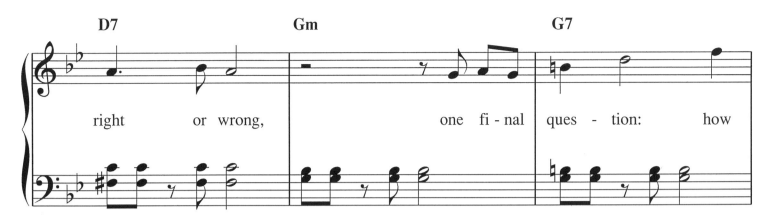

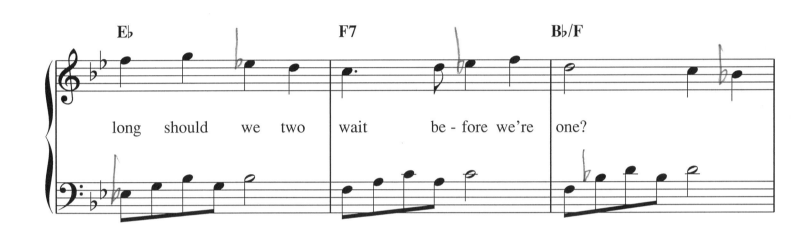

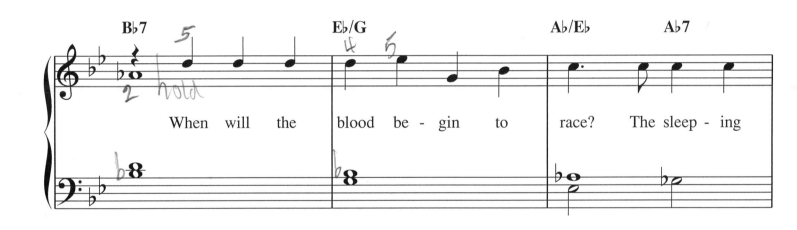

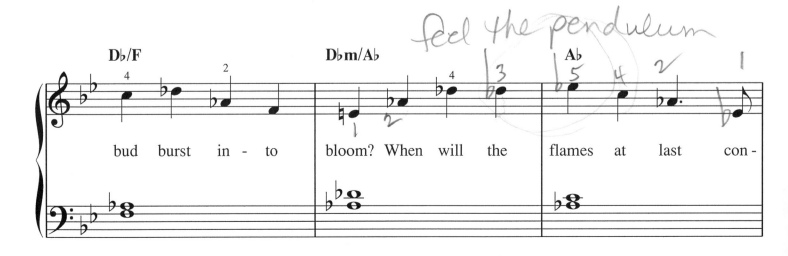

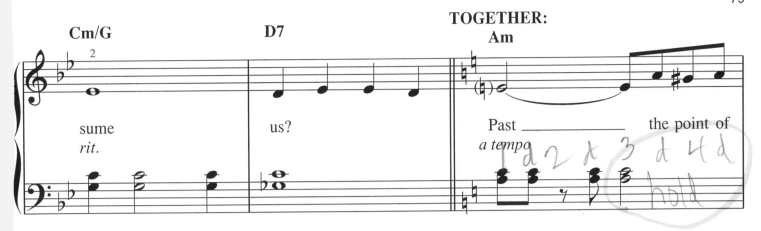

TOGETHER:

sume us? Past _____ the point of

rit. *a tempo*

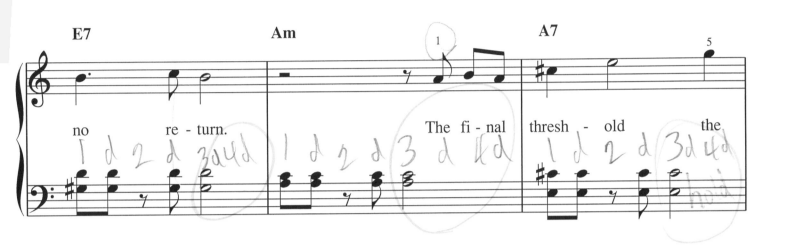

no re - turn. The fi - nal thresh - old the

bridge is crossed, so stand and watch it burn. _____ We've

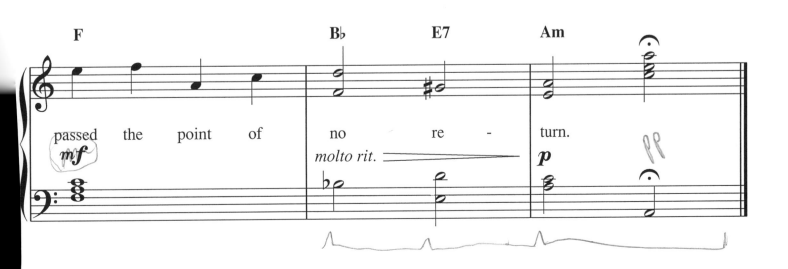

passed the point of no re - turn.

molto rit.

HAL•LEONARD™
CORPORATION
7777 W. BLUEMOUND RD. P.O. BOX 13819 MILWAUKEE, WI 53213

Photographs by Clive Barda
Cover artwork by Dewynters Limited, London

World premier at Her Majesty's Theatre
Thursday, October 9th, 1986